AF609374

AN OPINIONATED GUIDE

Photography

HOXTON MINI PRESS

Does

photography

matter?

'From today, painting is dead!' the French artist Paul Delaroche declared when he first set eyes on a photograph in around 1840.

Painting didn't perish under pressure from the new medium, of course, but Delaroche was hardly wrong in his estimation of photography's power to disrupt. Some considered it more science than art on the grounds that it was a mechanical process – and it was certainly used to settle essentially scientific questions, such as in Eadweard Muybridge's experiments with galloping animals.

But across the past two centuries artists have striven to develop its expressive as well as purely documentary potential, whether working in the studio like Andreas Sterzing and Cindy Sherman or the street like Joel Meyerowitz; whether drawing on techniques and ideas shared with the other arts like the Surrealist movement or unique to photography, as in Andreas Gursky's work; and whether, like Grace Robertson, aiming to capture a slice of reality or stage an alternate one, as in the work of Jeff Wall.

Photography is the most democratic of all artistic media. From the mid-19th century through to the advent of the digital age, it has continued to revolutionise the way people document their lives. So, yes, photography not only matters as a form of art and documentary; it is intrinsic to our everyday lives. The real question to ask is: in the smartphone-enabled, visually super-saturated present, given how busy we all are taking and sharing photographs, do we still have the time to actually look at them? This book is intended to encourage and help you to do just that.

The short story of photography

Two centuries ago, the secrets of 'writing with light' – the literal meaning of the word *photography* – were known only to a handful of inventor-initiates. Newspapers still illustrated their stories with hand-drawn images.

Galloping technological advances such as shortening exposure times, colour film and flash bulbs would change all that. Cameras would become increasingly sophisticated and portable, and war, motion, fashion, crime and the everyday life of the street would all be subjected to the photographer's gaze, sometimes analytical, sometimes playful.

Aesthetically, photography has passed through various phases and fashions: from soft-focus, self-consciously arty Pictorialism, through taken-on-the-fly street photography and 'decisive-moment' image-making, to staged photography, sometimes made with a budget that wouldn't look out of place on a Hollywood movie balance sheet.

Journalism would develop a new strand: photojournalism. Images could now take the lead in telling stories. And the equipment to take pictures would be put in everyone's hands: first through the democratising analogue innovations of the likes of Kodak and Polaroid, then through the advent of the digital smartphone, which has had an extraordinary impact. Few events – and non-events – are undocumented and unshared in the 21st century. What further changes will be wrought by the wide adoption of generative AI – freighted with both artistic opportunities and ethical quandaries – one can only wonder.

Snapshots of the history of photography

Camera obscura *500BCE–*

There has always been a need for realistic images of the world. The camera obscura involves passing light through a pinhole to project an image on the wall of a box or 'dark room' (the English meaning of the Latin term *camera obscura*), which can then be traced. It represents perhaps the earliest attempt to draw with light and appears to date back as far as 500BCE China.

The first photographs *1826–1839*

The early photographers were engineers and inventors rather than artists. The oldest known surviving camera photograph, *View from the Window at Le Gras*, taken in 1826, is a shadowy image requiring an exposure time of over eight hours – of interest now mostly for its technical accomplishment rather than any aesthetic quality. It wasn't until 19 August 1839 that photography was formally announced to the world. The invention was credited to Louis-Jacques-Mandé Daguerre, whose so-called 'daguerreotypes' required much-reduced exposure times – under 30 minutes – and were less susceptible to fading.

Photojournalism *1848–*

Photography is a great way to tell a story. It was first used to bring to life the words of an article in a French newspaper in 1848, and the practice grew increasingly popular in the following decades as the Crimean and American Civil Wars raged, with reporters sending images back from the battlefields (p.18). So-called 'photojournalism' would take new forms in the 20th century, when the invention of lighter, more portable cameras – such as the 35mm Leica – and the flash bulb, combined with the emergence of pioneering news magazines such as *Life* in America, *Vu* in France and *Picture Post* in the UK. These publications, which featured the work of photographers such as Henri Cartier-Bresson (p.30) and Grace Robertson (p.56), were more visually creative than newspapers, allowing images to take the lead in telling stories.

Pictorialism *1869–1920*

Initially, photography seemed to capture reality; as such, it wasn't particularly a medium for avowed 'artists'. But an international aesthetic movement known as Pictorialism emerged in the latter half of the 19th century that promoted painterly effects, achieved through manipulation of the negative and characterised by a self-consciously arty use of soft focus. The introduction of the first Kodak camera in 1888 significantly democratised the medium and meant that more or less everyone could now take photographs – 'You press the button, we do the rest', promised the advertising slogan. Setting themselves apart from these mere amateur snappers, 'true' artists embraced Pictorialism until the 1920s.

Fashion photography *1911–*

From the earliest days of the medium, Victorian ladies and gentlemen had enthusiastically posed for the camera in their smartest attire. But in 1911, Edward Steichen took what he declared 'the first serious fashion photographs ever made'. Steichen's images of models wearing designer dresses were published in French magazine *Art et Décoration* at the beginning of a new age of glamour which was being promoted in glossy fashion-focused magazines such as *Vogue*. The tradition instigated by Steichen ran on through the work of titans of the genre including Horst P. Horst, Cecil Beaton and Erwin Blumenfeld and continues today in the images of Tim Walker (p.118) and Ellen von Unwerth (p.114).

Surrealism *1924–*

Surrealism changed how artists depicted the world, prioritising dream logic and the unconscious over rationality. A number of photographic techniques are associated with the emergence of the movement in the wake of the publication of André Breton's first *Surrealist Manifesto* in 1924: photomontage, photograms (p.24) and solarisation among them. Key artists exploring these new processes and ways of seeing included Man Ray (p.32) and Lee Miller (p.44).

'The decisive moment' *1952*

There have been few more influential phrases in the history of photography than 'the decisive moment' – referring to the ability to select just the right nanosecond to release the camera shutter so that all the elements in the frame coalesce into a meaningful and geometrically satisfying composition, as in the image on page 30. That picture, taken by Henri Cartier-Bresson, seems an almost miraculous combination of spontaneous-looking action and formal perfection. As Cartier-Bresson explained in the introduction to his 1952 photobook, *Images à la Sauvette* (published in English under the title *The Decisive Moment*): 'Photography is the simultaneous recognition, in a fraction of a second, of the significance of an event as well as of a precise organisation of forms which give that event its proper expression.'

Entering the art world *1940–*

Can photography be 'art', or is its appeal too popular and its practice too widespread to justify that label? Museums and galleries were certainly slow to recognise the status of the 'new' medium. Photography was over a century old when, in 1940, the Museum of Modern Art (MoMA) in New York became the first major art museum to establish a department dedicated to it. A series of highly influential and unconventional photography shows followed, beginning with *The Family of Man* in 1955, which was curated by Edward Steichen and featured 503 photographs from 273 different photographers, including Dorothea Lange (p.38), Bill Brandt (p.40) and Helen Levitt (p.86). Optimistic and universalist in theme – 68 countries were represented – it displayed most of the images unframed and collaged or suspended in mid-air. By the time it had completed a tour of six continents, the show had reached an estimated audience of more than 10 million – so proving that photography could be both art *and* popular.

Street photography *1967–*

The tradition of street photography – that is, 'candid pictures of everyday life in the street', according to Colin Westerbeck and Joel Meyerowitz in their history of the genre – dates back at least as far as the work of Eugène Atget (1857–1927). It was given fresh life in the 1960s by a group of New York photographers, including Meyerowitz himself (p.68) and Garry Winogrand (p.64), whose reputation was sealed thanks to his inclusion in *New Documents*, an epoch-making photography exhibition at MoMA in 1967 that canonised a more personal and snapshot-like approach to documentary photography.

Art embraces colour *1976–*

The use of colour in art photography has a tortured history. Eminent photographers such as Walker Evans had declared it 'vulgar', and the gallery and museum world generally made a distinction between amateur or commercial photographers, who operated in colour, and artists bearing cameras, who worked in black and white. A watershed moment came in 1975, when MoMA put on an exhibition of prints by William Eggleston (p.66). The following year it staged a show by Stephen Shore (p.70), another 'member of the new generation of colour photographers', as the museum declared, signalling that the art world was finally embracing the use of colour in art photography.

Düsseldorf School *1980s–*

Photographic prints grew a lot bigger in size around the turn of the millennium, with large-format architectural shots such as Andreas Gursky's *Shanghai* (3.01 × 2.06 m; p.108) dominating vast expanses of wall space in galleries and museums. Gursky studied in Düsseldorf with the husband-and-wife duo Bernd and Hilla Becher, whose black-and-white images showing industrial structures and machinery such as kilns and blast furnaces had launched a new conceptual photographic movement known as the Düsseldorf School, after the Kunstakademie Düsseldorf in Germany where they taught. Technological advances have allowed the couple's artistic heirs to display their work at ever greater scale.

Staged photography *1990s–*

Photographers often document reality as they find it, but they are also sometimes tempted to construct their own reality to photograph. This requires time, effort and money, of course, but the increasing commercial success of art photography and the technical ability to produce ever larger pin-sharp prints helped to make the creation of incredibly elaborate staged photography viable. As the 20th century drew to a close, photographers like Jeff Wall (p.104) and Gregory Crewdson began to work more in the manner of Hollywood film directors, spending significant budgets and building their own sets.

Smartphone *2000–*

The introduction of the camera phone further democratised photography, both amateur and professional. It was a sign of the shifting times when, in 2004, Kodak discontinued the manufacture of film cameras. By 2012, when the prestigious

US publication *Time* put an iPhone image on the cover of its print magazine, the quality of the images being shot on smartphones could no longer be denied. The photograph was taken by the acclaimed war photographer Benjamin Lowy, who began his career using analogue cameras before becoming an early proponent of phone photography.

Post-photography *2010–*

Art history is forever asking the question: what follows after this? After Impressionism came Post-Impressionism; after modernism came postmodernism. Post-photography is an as yet ill-defined term that can be deployed to describe a variety of different trends in the age of the ubiquitous digital image. One important strand has artists using photographs – sometimes their own original images, sometimes borrowed images – to combine the products of the camera eye with other techniques, such as embroidery (p.140), which turn photographs, so readily shared online, into avowedly physical and unique objects.

Artificial intelligence *2020s–*

While AI-generated images have been around for decades, it was not until the 2020s when they became sophisticated enough to enter the public consciousness. Now, AI is further redefining the boundaries of photography, enhancing pre-existing images or creating entirely new ones. The future for AI-enhanced photography is either bright or dark, depending on who you speak to. The truth is, no one truly knows – the picture remains blurry.

Where can I see it?

Victoria and Albert Museum

London / vam.ac.uk

The V&A began collecting photographs in the 1850s – the museum's first director, Henry Cole, was himself a keen snapper – and now houses one of the largest archives in the world, running from Julia Margaret Cameron through to Martin Parr (p.98). The recent addition of material from the National Media Museum in Bradford has further enriched the collection.

The Photographers' Gallery

London / thephotographersgallery.org.uk

Founded in 1971 and housed on the edge of Soho since 2012, this is one of the best places to discover great contemporary photography in London. There are exhibitions, talks and courses, as well as a shop, prints sales gallery and nice cafe.

Paris Photo

Paris / parisphoto.com

Photo fairs are a great place to discover both classic and contemporary photography. One of the best remains Paris Photo, founded in 1997 and held annually in November, usually in the Grand Palais on the Champs-Elysées. There is an accompanying exhibition and talks programme, and the Offprint book fair is held simultaneously nearby.

Foam

Amsterdam / foam.org

Foam (or Fotografiemuseum Amsterdam) opened on the Keizersgracht in 2001 and mounts an ambitious exhibition programme, as well as publishing an influential quarterly publication, *Foam Magazine*. Each September, Amsterdam is also home to the leading international photography art fair, Unseen.

Museum für Fotografie

Berlin / smb.museum

Famed for its fashion collection, Berlin's Museum of Photography opened in 2004 and houses the Helmut Newton Foundation and the permanent exhibition Helmut Newton's Private Property, which includes Newton's cameras, library and parts of his Monte Carlo office. (For an example of Newton's work, see p.74.)

Museum of Modern Art

New York / moma.org

MoMA began to collect photographs in 1930 and established a dedicated photography department in 1940. Across the decades, it has staged some of the most epoch-defining photographic shows, beginning with The Family of Man in 1955. Its collection of more than 25,000 images includes work by Man Ray (p.32), Bill Brandt (p.40) and Dorothea Lange (p.38).

International Center of Photography

New York / icp.org

The ICP was founded in 1974 by Cornell Capa, Hungarian-American photographer and brother of war photographer

Robert Capa, with the goal of championing 'concerned photography' – social and political images that might change and improve the world. It has a large collection of magazines from the first part of the 20th century, and the School at ICP runs an educational programme.

George Eastman Museum

Rochester, New York / eastman.org

George Eastman was the founder of Eastman Kodak, a company more or less synonymous with the history of photography. It's therefore appropriate that a museum bearing his name and based in Rochester, New York, the city that is home to Kodak's headquarters, should contain one of the largest collections of work in the world, with 19th-century holdings including photographs by Timothy O'Sullivan (p.18) and Eadweard Muybridge (p.20)

Museum of Contemporary Photography

Chicago / mocp.org

Founded in 1976 by Columbia College Chicago, the MoCP is known for launching the careers of budding photographers, including Alec Soth (p.112). It has a comprehensive collection of over 16,000 images from over 1,500 photographers from around the world.

Tokyo Photographic Museum

Tokyo / topmuseum.jp

The Tokyo Photographic Museum curates thematic exhibitions from its vast collection of over 37,000 images, as well as showcasing individual photographers from Japan and beyond.

Contributors

Robert Shore has written a number of books about art and photography: *Post-Photography* (2014), *Beg, Steal and Borrow* (2017), *Andy Warhol* (2020), *Yayoi Kusama* (2021) and (with Joel Meyerowitz) *Joel Meyerowitz: A Question of Color* (2023). He was formerly the deputy editor of *Art Review* magazine and creative director of *Elephant*.

Hoxton Mini Press is a small independent publisher from east London. We believe in books. We believe in beautiful books. We believe in beautiful books that can be collected on nice wooden shelves and kept for future generations. We also plant loads of trees.

About the series

In an age when everything can be researched online we believe that strong opinion is better than more information. The intention of these 'opinionated' guides is not to tell you everything but to spark curiosity in the subject and, just maybe, lift your day a little.

Artworks

TIMOTHY H. O'SULLIVAN

A Harvest of Death, Gettysburg, Pennsylvania, 1863

War photography pioneer looks death in the face

This photograph of dead soldiers awaiting burial after the Battle of Gettysburg, a bloody turning point in the American Civil War, is the first image of its kind. In contrast to the triumphant pageantry and propagandistic staged scenes of army life that had typified earlier depictions of war, Timothy H. O'Sullivan's photograph offers up the stark reality of the killing fields, what American poet Oliver Wendell Holmes called 'wrecks of manhood'. The battle lasted three days, and over 50,000 soldiers died. O'Sullivan was one of many Northern men who gained prominence as war photographers of the Civil War, unflinchingly documenting the horrors of what many initially considered a great adventure. The title of the image, with its poetic juxtaposition, is significant: the dead men are a macabre harvest, and they too have been harvested, their pockets turned inside out, their boots and guns removed – resources are scarce. The contrast between the pin-sharp clarity of the foreground and the eerie haziness of the receding landscape, with its ghostlike silhouette of a man on horseback, suggests a distant hinterland of bodies, of which we only see a few.

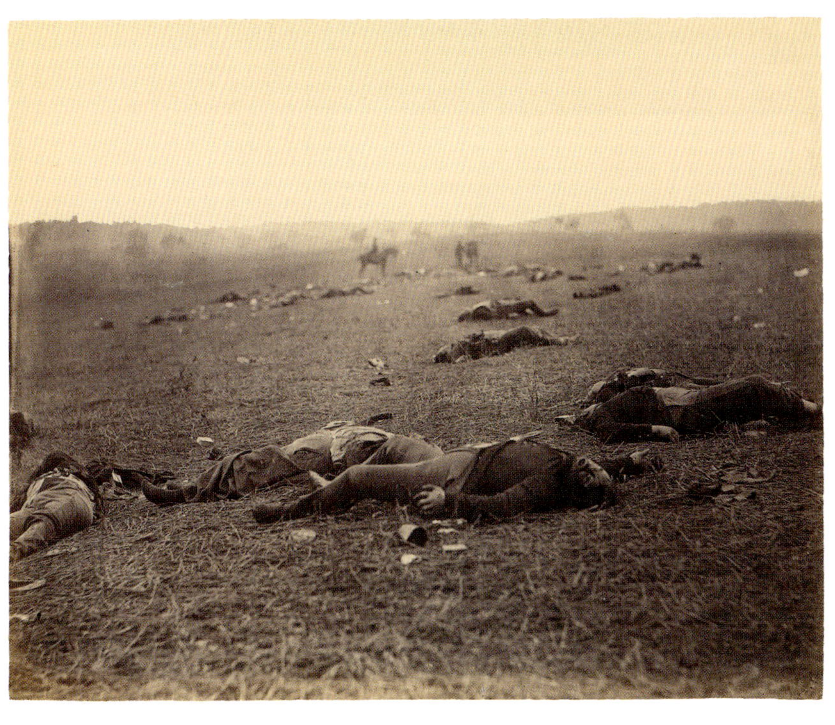

Timothy H. O'Sullivan, *A Harvest of Death*, Gettysburg, Pennsylvania, 1863, albumen silver print from a glass negative, Metropolitan Museum of Art, New York

EADWEARD MUYBRIDGE

Cat; Trotting; Change to Galloping, 1872–85

Man splices time, makes motion visible

Is it art? Is it science? It's both. In 1872, to settle once and for all the question of whether a horse's four legs did in fact clear the ground simultaneously during a gallop, Eadweard Muybridge invented a way of capturing different animals in motion to make visible what had previously been only a blur. No single camera was fast enough to achieve this, so Muybridge set up a whole battery of them with specially designed shutters that would each capture a tiny fraction of movement, triggered by a series of trip-wires to produce a sequence spun from thin slices of time. Now you see it: a galloping four-legged creature is indeed briefly airborne (it is a cat rather than a horse, here, as images of the latter in motion have become overfamiliar whereas cats retain their mystery). The 20 exposures arranged in a grid aim for maximum scientific objectivity, and to this day Muybridge's photographs help us to understand and visualise the reality of motion. But they also paved the way for artists like Marcel Duchamp to explore the uncanny nature of repetition and distortion in paintings such as *Nude Descending a Staircase (No. 2)*, 1912.

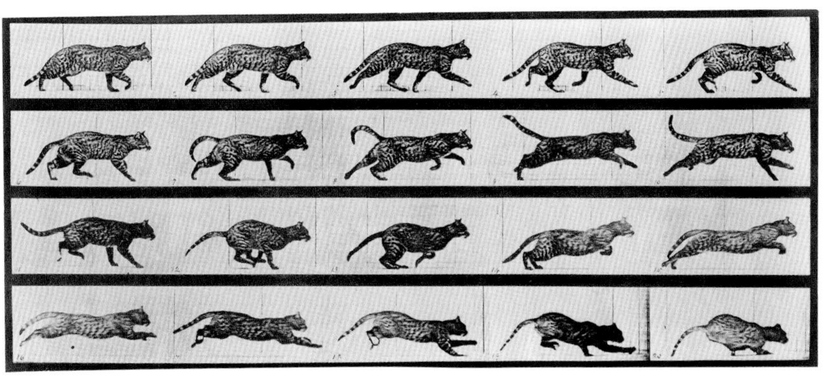

Eadweard Muybridge, *Cat; Trotting; Change to Galloping*, 1872–85, collotype on white wove paper, Royal Academy, London

JACQUES-HENRI LARTIGUE

Grand Prix of the Automobile Club of France, 1912

Standing eye to eye with speed

Jacques-Henri Lartigue's lifelong fascination with automobiles – and all other kinetic, beautiful, modern things – started at a very young age, and he began to photograph racing cars as soon as he was able to, in his twenties. This astonishing image, a technical experiment in capturing speed on film, was taken standing on the very edge of the road as the car raced past Lartigue at 140km/h. Lartigue pivoted slightly while shooting in order to keep the vehicle in his sights, attempting to merge with the motion itself. The extreme velocity is palpable: the car's tyres look as though they're being stretched, cartoon-like, and the silhouettes of the spectators across the road are also distorted, like violently windswept grasses. We can almost feel the vivid sensations experienced by Lartigue, imagining that the car was carrying him away with its momentum as it whizzed past. Human faces blur into insignificance.

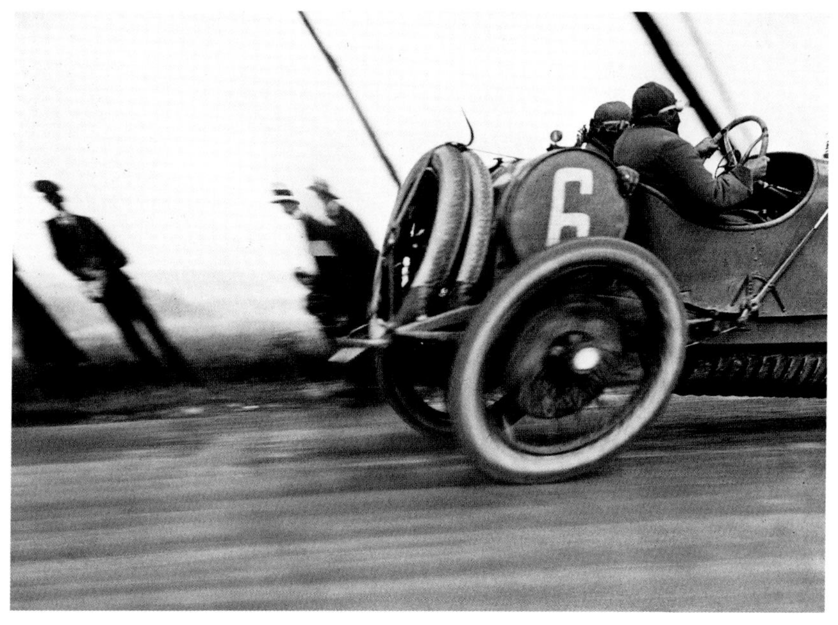

Jacques-Henri Lartigue, *Grand Prix of the Automobile Club of France, Course à Dieppe*, 1912

LÁZLÓ MOHOLY-NAGY

Photogram, 1926

Photographer paints with light

This image was made without a camera, simply by placing objects – a metal grid and a paint brush – alongside the artist's hand on paper coated with a photosensitive chemical. The light cast on the arrangement captures the objects' silhouette in negative. There is something quasi-scientific about this ghostly trace, like an X-ray. A key figure of the Bauhaus, a German school that sought to combine art, design and architecture, Hungarian painter and photographer Moholy-Nagy pursued his experimental photogram project for 20 years, recapturing and updating a picture-making process dating back to the 19th-century founders of photography. What's revolutionary here is that he is trying to shape light with objects, rather than the other way around. To Moholy-Nagy – a modernist fascinated with technology and machinery – light was the new medium, even a new sort of pigment. This image, containing as it does the artist's hand and his brush, feels like an abstract representation of painting, bringing a traditional art form into the new century. By making his own hand one of the components, Moholy-Nagy turns the image into a sly self-portrait, putting himself and his artistic practice at the heart of it.

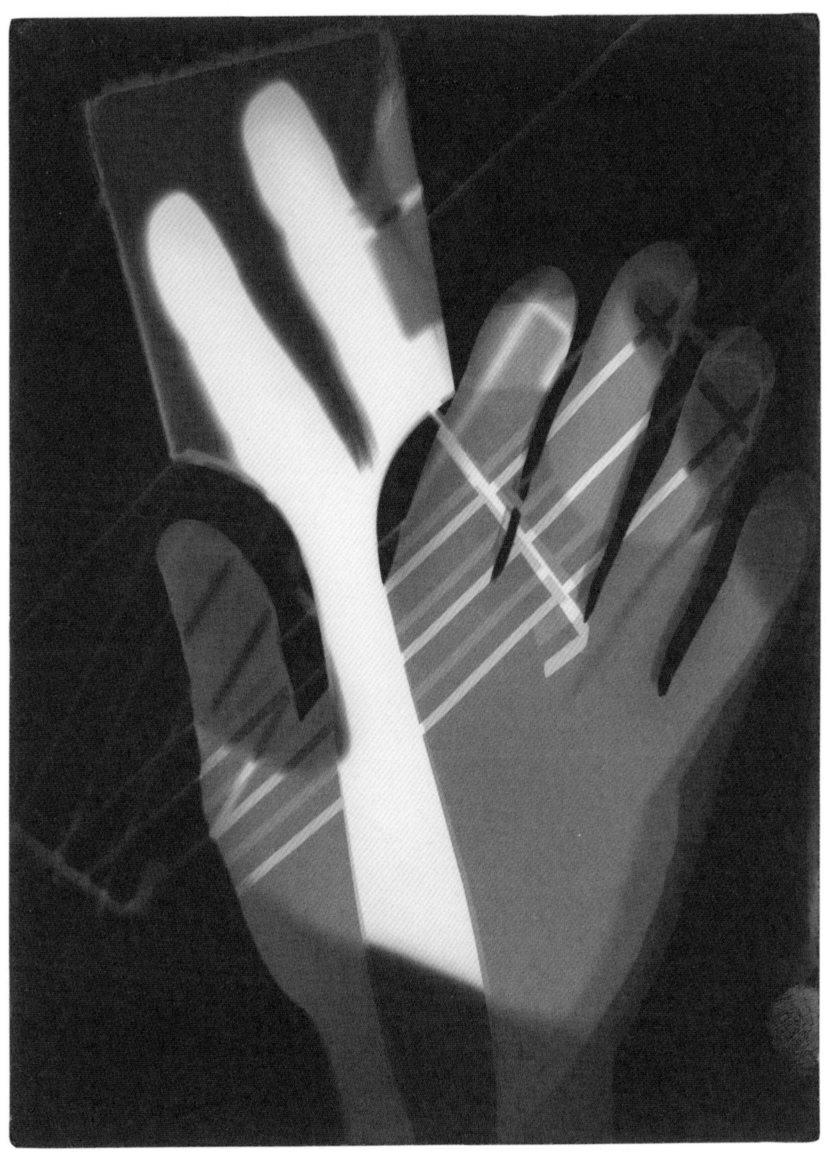

Lázló Moholy-Nagy, *Photogram*, 1926, gelatin silver photogram

ANDRÉ KERTÉSZ

Champs-Elysées, 1929

An outsider conjures presence through absence

André Kertész relocated to Paris from Hungary in 1925 and, speaking little French, walked the streets of the city alone as a foreigner-flâneur, bearing a small 35mm camera. In his meanderings, he spent a lot of time in parks, which, with their profusion of benches and chairs, serve as vast outdoor sitting rooms for city-dwellers. Here there are no people, only furniture designed for their use, and the chairs' projected shadows. 'You don't see the things you photograph, you feel them,' Kertész said. And we in turn feel several things at once. There is elegance and poetry in this Parisian staging of modern urban life. There is melancholy, but without inertia: the composition of the row of chairs has rhythm. Was it Kertész who turned one of the chairs to face the other way, or did he find the arrangement ready-made? The crowd of chairs, waiting, also anticipates Eugène Ionesco's 1952 Absurdist play *Les Chaises*, where chairs mysteriously proliferate on the stage. Kertész's many photographs of empty chairs (they were a recurring subject for the photographer) are more than just pieces of empty furniture, they signal a shift in European thought: this is urban still life as meditation.

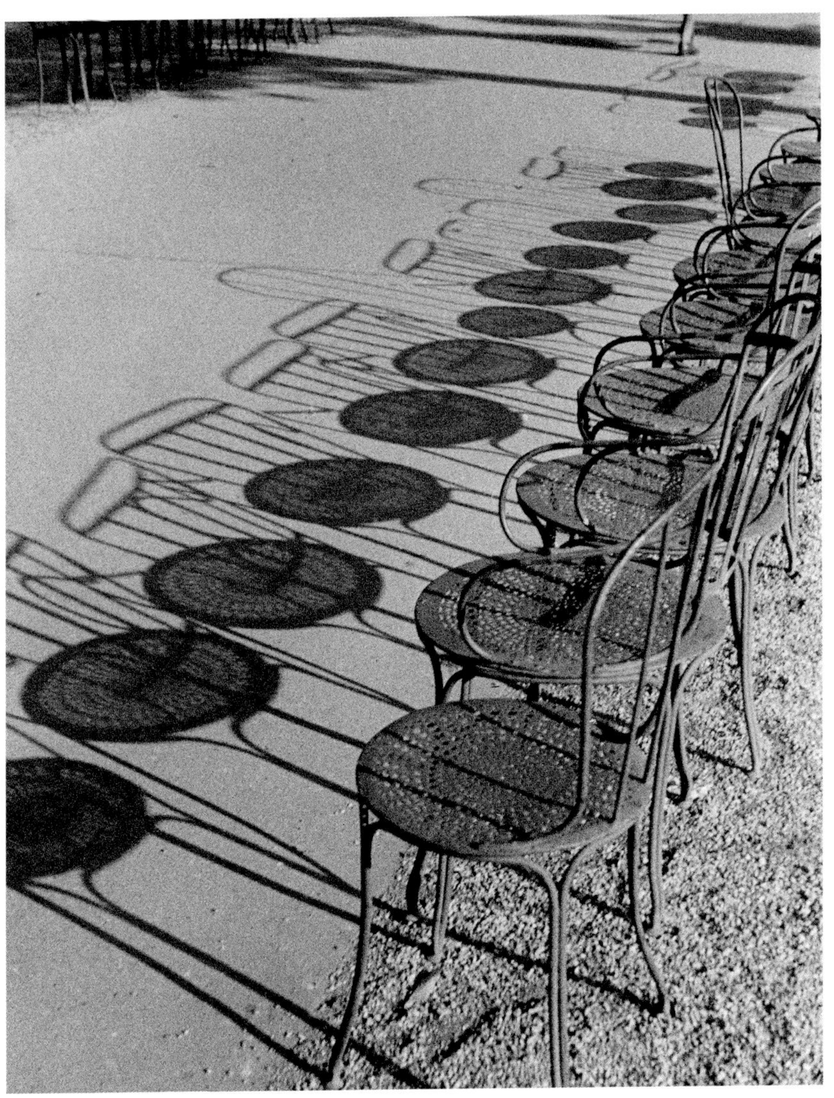

André Kertész, *Champs-Elysées*, 1929

CLAUDE CAHUN

Self-Portrait, from *Bifur*, No 5, 1930

Artist of the self strips to enigmatic core

'Under this mask, another mask,' declared artist and writer Claude Cahun. 'I will never be finished removing all these faces.' Born in 1894, Lucy Schwob changed her name to the gender-neutral Claude Cahun in 1918, when she started to make photographic self-portraits. Here, she is 36 and living openly in Paris with her lover and artistic partner Marcel Moore (born Suzanne Malherbe). Rather than a fully-fledged member of the Surrealist movement – 'Labels are despicable,' she said – Cahun was surrealist by nature, a dissident who used photography as a form of masquerade to explore her androgyny. Compared to other works by her that involve props or photomontage, this challenging image is one of her most pared-down. The shaved head and eyebrows are a radical act of defiance; looking down, she withholds her gaze. The artist's self is concealed within, in the depths beyond the pale skull and the dark recesses of eyes and mouth. Cahun described her exploration of self as a 'hunt' – this image suggests both inquiry and deathly pursuit. Cahun inspired the self-portraits of Cindy Sherman (p.76) and Nan Goldin. David Bowie, a man of many faces himself, was also a fan.

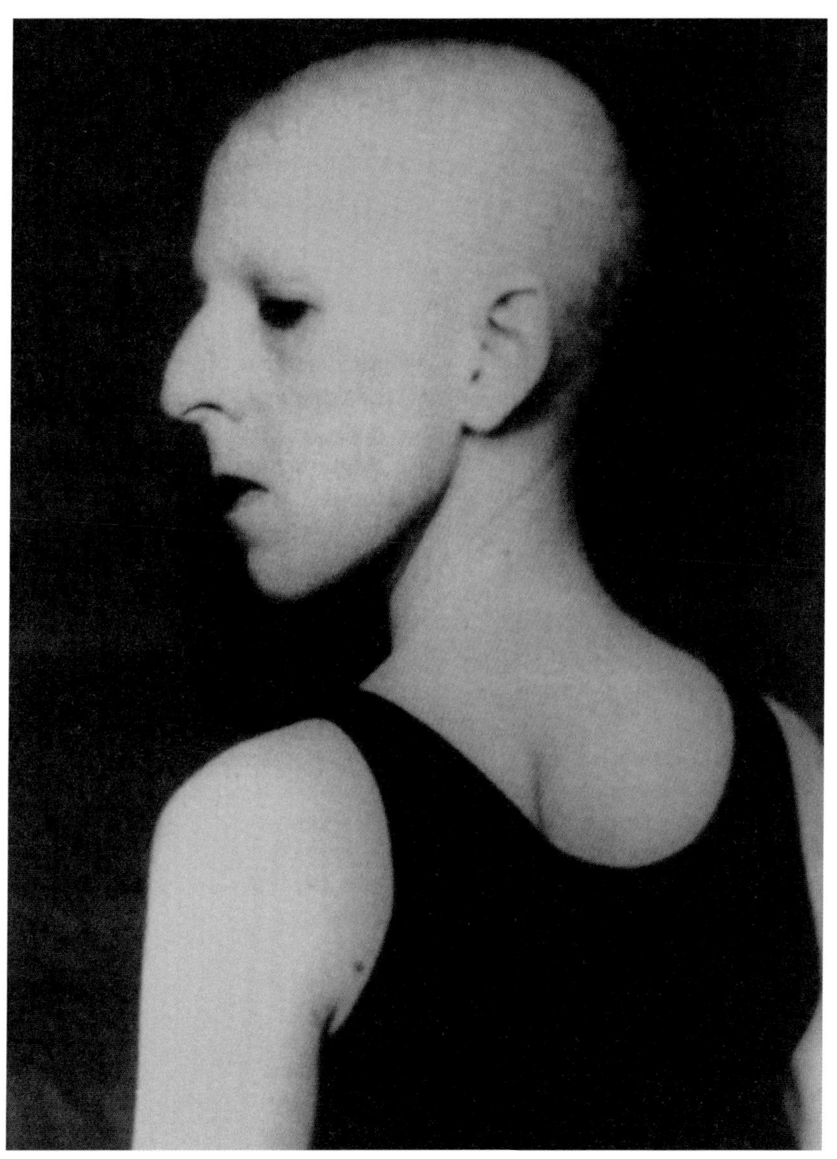

Claude Cahun, *Self-Portrait, from Bifur, No 5*, 1930, Editions du Carrefour, Paris (repository)

HENRI CARTIER-BRESSON

Behind the Gare St-Lazare, 1932

Time freezes when man shoots man mid-leap

Describing the perfect photograph, the Surrealist André Breton said it was 'shadow and prey mingled in a unique flash'. In 1932, Henri Cartier-Bresson captured his shadow/prey – this rapturous image of a leaping stranger mid-flight – when leaning on a fence overlooking a partially flooded building site. He had spent the previous year working as a hunter in Côte d'Ivoire in French colonial Africa, going out at night with a gun and a head torch. Back in Europe, a small hand-held Leica allowed Cartier-Bresson to achieve pioneering feats of on-the-fly snapshot photography that would have been impossible with a large stationary camera on a tripod. The camera (which he wrapped in black tape to camouflage it) became his eye, while his constant state of being as a flâneur (an acute observer of modern life strolling through the streets of the city), as with hunting, was a combination of hyper-alertness and patience. In this image, lines, curves and shapes come together; reflected in the mirror-like surface of the water are the leaping man and, behind him, delightfully, a poster advertising a Russian circus displays an image of a leaping dancer. Life imitates art, for a split second and forever.

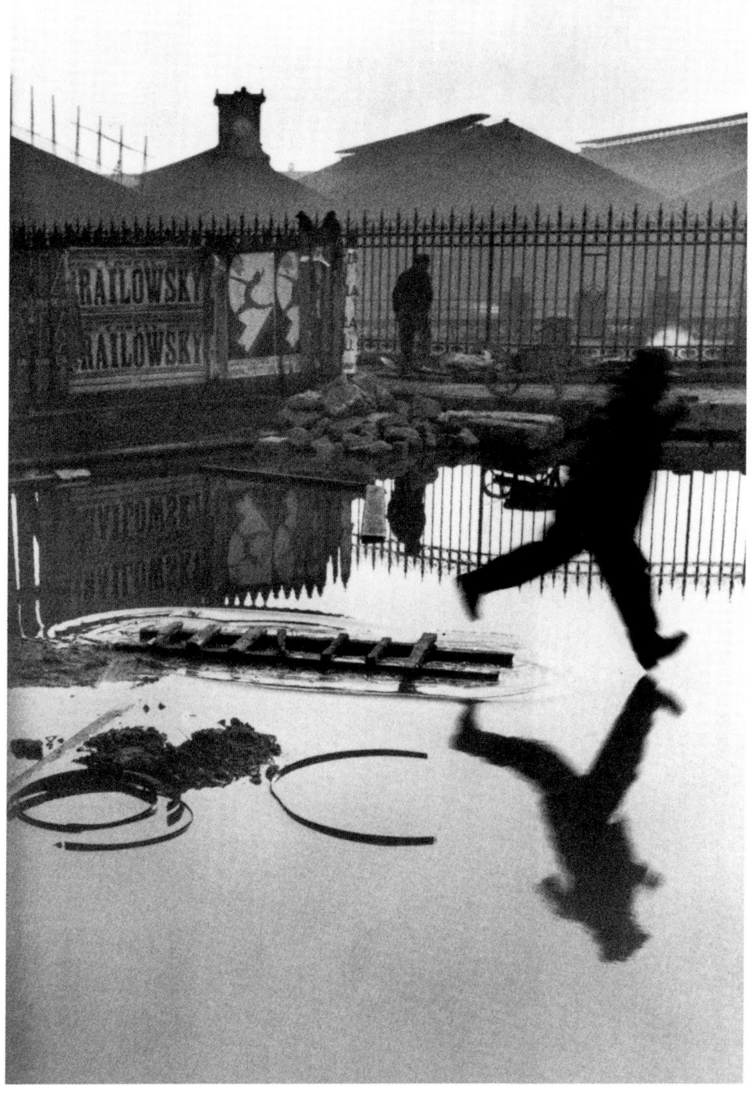

Henri Cartier-Bresson, *Behind the Gare St-Lazare*, 1932, gelatin silver print, printed 1950s, Museum of Modern Art, New York

MAN RAY

Les larmes (Glass Tears), 1932

Surreal advert captures quintessence of artifice

This stunning image of artifice by American Dada and Surrealist artist Man Ray started out as an ad for Cosmecil mascara. 'Madame, cry at the cinema, cry at the theatre, laugh until you cry, without fearing for your beautiful eyes': so ran the copy for the waterproof product, which came in 11 different shades. What makes this close-up of a model (and French can-can dancer) more than a commercial image, but a work of art as well? Its wildly exaggerated glamour – the elongated eyelashes with their droplet-like tips, the thin pencilled eyebrows, the eyes gazing dramatically heavenward – gestures towards the expressionist acting of a silent movie star reaching a melodramatic climax. The perfectly spherical tears (not glass but glycerin) stuck to the model's face are obviously, triumphantly, fake. The iconic *Glass Tears* followed closely behind the visceral 'sliced eyeball' scene from Luis Buñuel's 1929 film, *Un Chien Andalou*: the eye, a physical portal, was a central motif in Surrealism's unsettling exploration of the liminal territory between dream and reality.

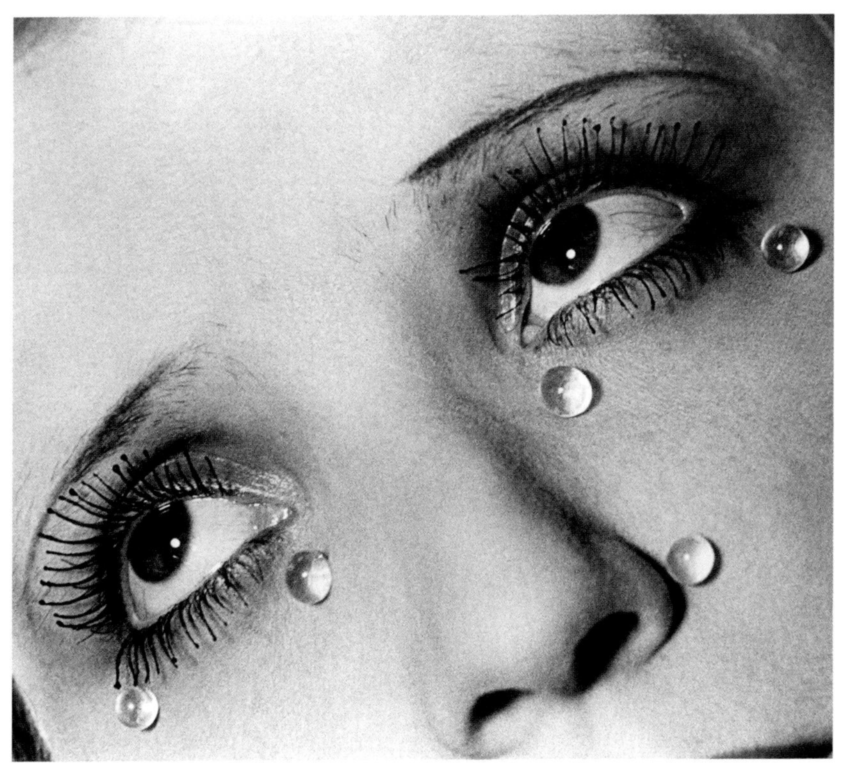

Man Ray, *Les larmes (Glass Tears)*, 1932, gelatin silver print, 22.9 × 29.8 cm, J. Paul Getty Museum, Los Angeles

Mrs Michael Balcon as Minerva, 1935

Colour pioneer reinvents the society portrait

Partly inspired by the Olympian Ball held at Claridge's Hotel in 1935, Madame Yevonde's *Goddesses* studio series portrays 1930s British society beauties transmogrified into figures from classical mythology. A suffragette in her youth, Yevonde set up a photographic studio to achieve financial independence and believed strongly in the importance of women's contribution to photography. At a time when colour was thought only good for advertising, she used the British print process Vivex to achieve a heightened colour palette. This otherworldly composition is one of her most accomplished and illustrates her inventive Surrealist/modernist sensibility. Portrayed as Minerva, Goddess of War, Aileen Balcon is shot against a dark background suggesting rocky terrain, perhaps even wartime trenches. But the lighting is improbably gorgeous, and Balcon's carefully made-up face, painted nails and the elegant gold drapery of her gown are juxtaposed with the modern helmet and – instead of the goddess's spear – revolver of a World War I soldier, forging a new female mythology. Next to her are her owl – symbol of wisdom – and a history of England, drawing a line between classical myth and England poised between the wars.

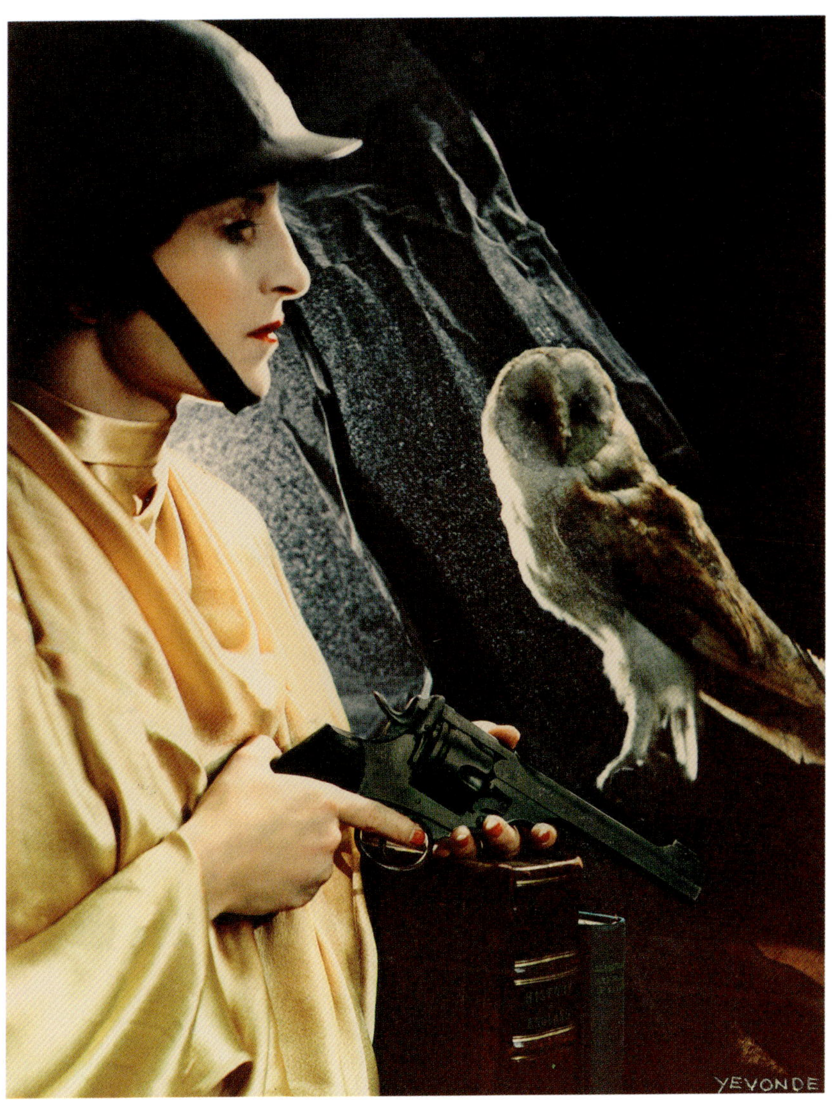

Madame Yevonde, *Mrs Michael Balcon as Minerva*, June 1935, Vivex colour print, 34.2 × 27 cm, The Laing Art Gallery, Newcastle-upon-Tyne

EDWARD WESTON

Nude (Charis, Santa Monica), 1936

Man with camera sculpts his lover with light

Weston's images are characteristically pared down and purified, which is as true of his nudes as his photographs of seashells and sand dunes. Here, his muse Charis Wilson sits with her arms wrapped around her knees, forming an elegant composition of planes and curves evocative of a modernist sculpture. Her face is hidden, eliminating personal characteristics and keeping the focus on the form. But the image also captures a moment of close intimacy. We are acutely aware of the heat of the sun (Charis has just turned her face away to avoid being dazzled), of the texture of the blanket she is sitting on, of the uneven parting of her hair on her pebble-smooth head and of the variations in her skin tone in the light and shade. 'The camera should be used for a recording of life,' Weston said, 'for rendering the very substance and quintessence of the thing itself, whether it be polished steel or palpitating flesh.'

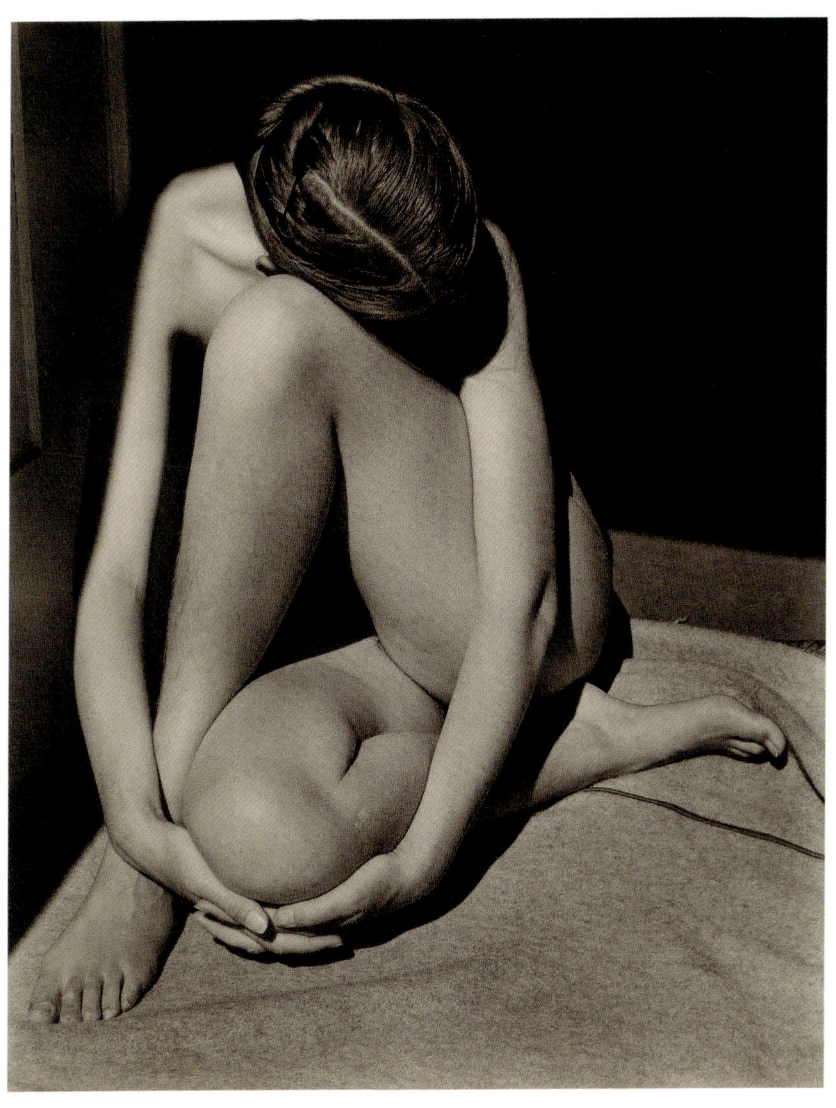

Edward Weston, *Nude (Charis, Santa Monica)*, 1936, gelatin silver print, 24.1 × 19.2 cm

DOROTHEA LANGE

Migrant Mother, Nipomo, California, 1936

Poster girl of the Great Depression

Soon after the 1929 Wall Street Crash triggered the Great Depression, a severe drought ravaged millions of acres of farmland and the soil in the prairie states turned to dust. Hundreds of thousands fled towards California and Dorothea Lange was one of the photographers appointed by the Farm Security Administration (FSA) to capture moving portraits of the migrants in support of President Roosevelt's New Deal economic relief policies. In 1936, she almost drove past a pea-pickers camp without stopping, before changing her mind and going to have a look around: 'I saw and approached the hungry and desperate mother, as if drawn by a magnet,' she recounted, using the language of destiny. Sitting under a makeshift tent, the 32-year-old Florence Thompson explained that she and her children had been living off frozen vegetables they dug out of the surrounding fields. Lange's portrait of her was distributed to newspapers across the United States. It quickly and – upsettingly for its subject, who saw it as a humiliating curse – definitively became an icon of poverty and maternal fortitude, perhaps because of Thompson's handsome, expressive face. Perhaps also because, with her baby in her arms, she looks like a modern-day Madonna.

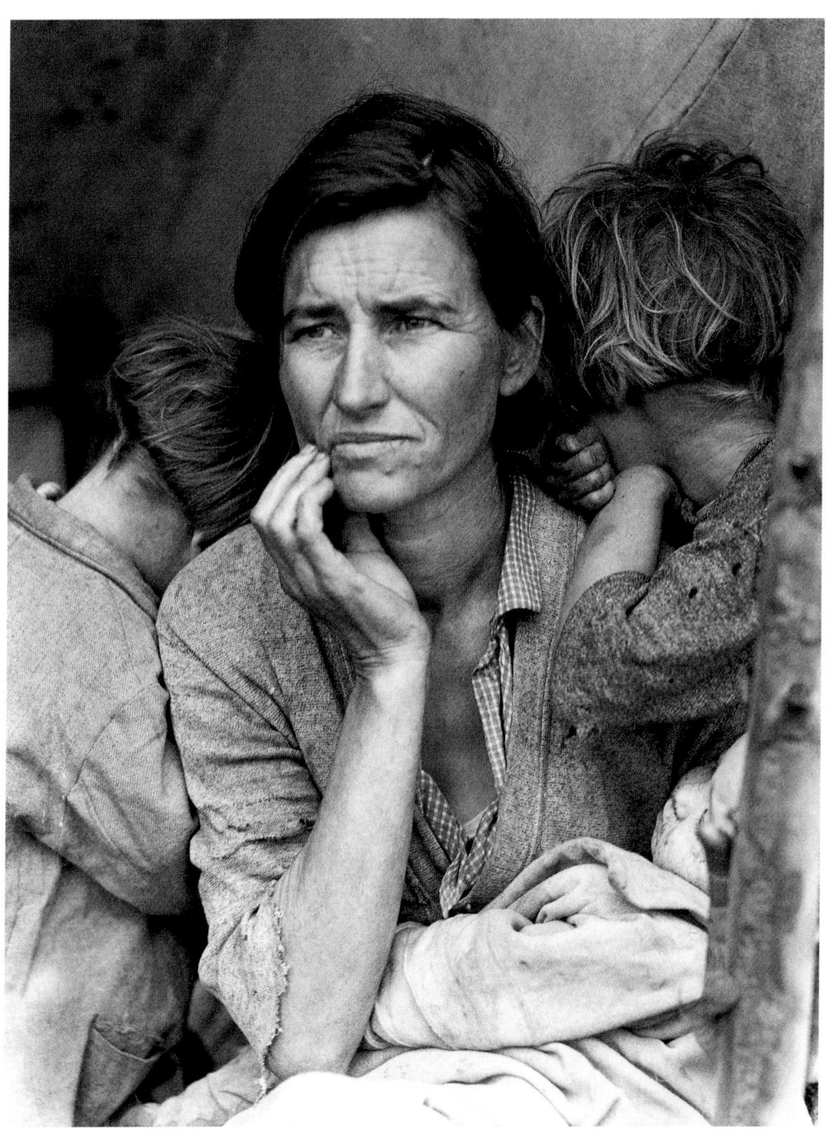

Dorothea Lange, *Migrant Mother, Nipomo, California*, 1936, gelatin silver print, 28.3 × 21.8 cm, Los Angeles County Museum of Art

BILL BRANDT

A Snicket in Halifax, 1937

Simple street scene distils fascination with the strange

German-born photographer Bill Brandt developed his distinctive vision in England, where he settled after a formative stint in Paris working with the Surrealist Man Ray (p.32). Like André Kertész (p.26) before him in Paris, Brandt brought to his adopted home the estranging gaze of an émigré outsider. He visited Yorkshire at a time of crisis in the mining and steel industries, witnessing extraordinary scenes of deprivation. This is an image of the industrial town of Halifax. The building on the left, with its blind windows and plume of smoke or smog, looks like a factory; the snicket, a Northern English word for a narrow alleyway, is most likely a route used by workers. At the same time, devoid of human presence, cropped and shot at an unusual angle that makes the perspective vertiginous, the image heightens ordinary reality, imbuing it with a nightmarish, uncanny atmosphere. For Brandt, this possibly captures the essence of the place; another image in the same series is entitled *Hail Hell or Halifax*. It also transforms the street scene, with its road rising into the suggested void beyond – a modernist stage set for an existentialist play.

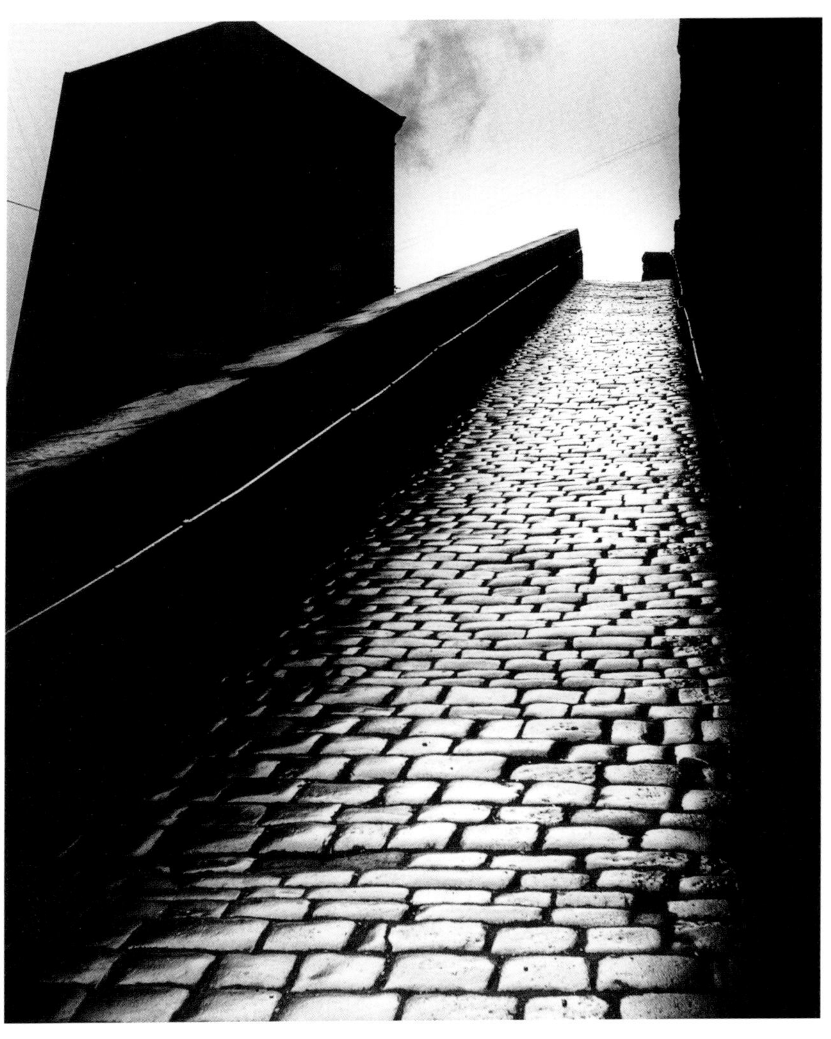

Bill Brandt, *A Snicket in Halifax*, 1937, gelatin silver print, 51 × 43.7 cm, Philadelphia Museum of Art

WEEGEE

On the Spot, 1939

Darker than film noir: real life and real death

The clammy air of menace in this image is pure film noir. Here is Gotham City – the New York of mobsters and their gangs of hired killers. We might expect the appearance of a hard-boiled private eye played by Humphrey Bogart. In fact, this isn't a still from a Hollywood movie, but a real-life picture taken by tabloid photographer Weegee (born Arthur Fellig). He worked at night, documenting murders, fires and car crashes and creating a completely new photographic genre in the process. Weegee's nickname was allegedly inspired by the Ouija board, because of his uncanny ability to appear on the scene of a tragedy before other reporters. In this, Weegee was helped by the fact that he lived behind the Manhattan Police HQ and had a shortwave police radio in his car. He had the ability, as evidenced here, to document a crime scene factually while allowing a significant composition to form before his camera. The title, *On the Spot*, refers to the police officers' presence at the scene, but it is also the prophetic name of the bar in front of which the man was shot; the spot pictured on the sign mirrored in the blood spilling darkly on the ground.

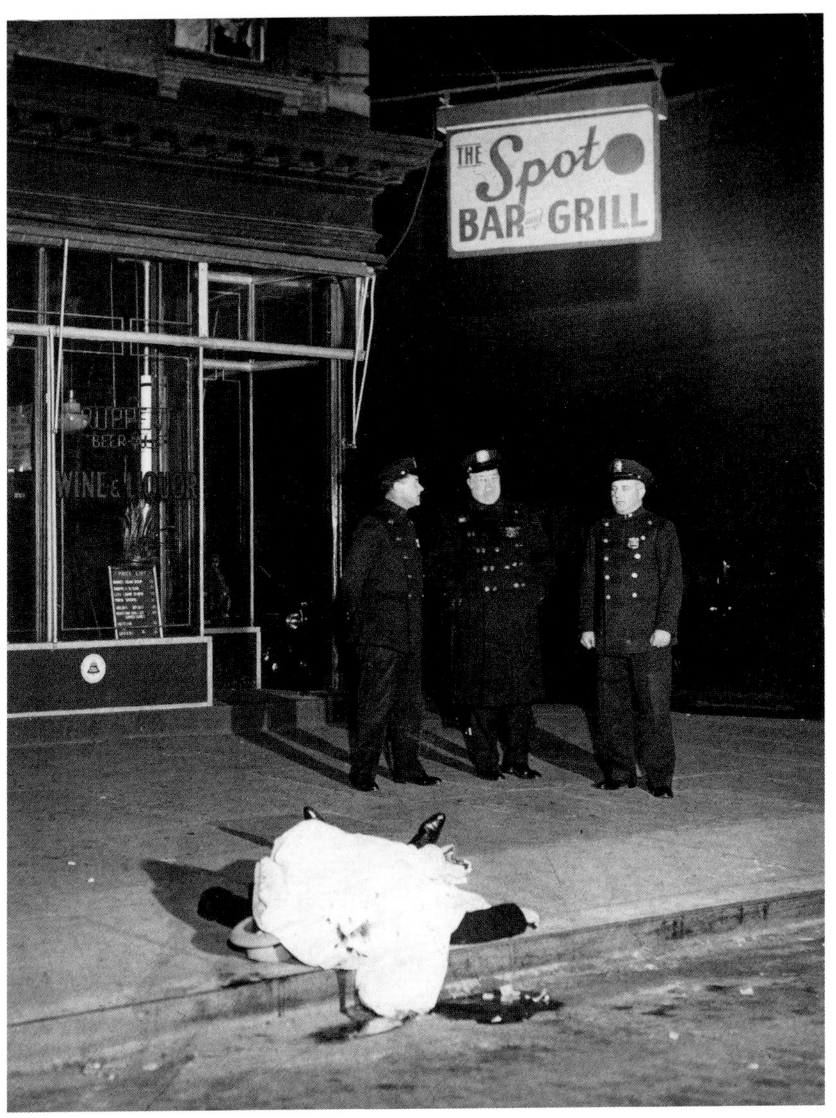

Weegee, *On the Spot*, 1939, gelatin silver print, 14 × 11 cm

LEE MILLER

David E. Scherman, Dressed for War, 1942

Model-turned-reporter shoots reporter-turned-model

'I'd rather take a picture than be one,' Lee Miller said when she switched careers from modelling to photojournalism. During World War II, Miller became a war correspondent for *Vogue* and teamed up with *Life* magazine reporter David E. Scherman. Together, they followed the US Army as it advanced through occupied France, engaging in siege warfare that reminded Miller of 'crusader times'. Though the subject of the photo is Scherman, this is also an oblique self-portrait of Miller: she too was dressed for war, one of only a few female photographers working as official war correspondents. Miller had worked with Man Ray in the 1930s and here she brings a Surrealist's eye to documentary work. The dehumanising effect of Scherman's face encased in his gas mask and steel helmet is juxtaposed with a jaunty striped umbrella, a piece of photographic equipment that also hints at the pleasures of the beach. After modelling, Miller was now recalibrating her approach in keeping with the harsh realities of war. She would document the chaos following D-Day, the Liberation of Paris and the US Army's entry into the concentration camps of Buchenwald and Dachau, producing some of the first photographic evidence of the Holocaust.

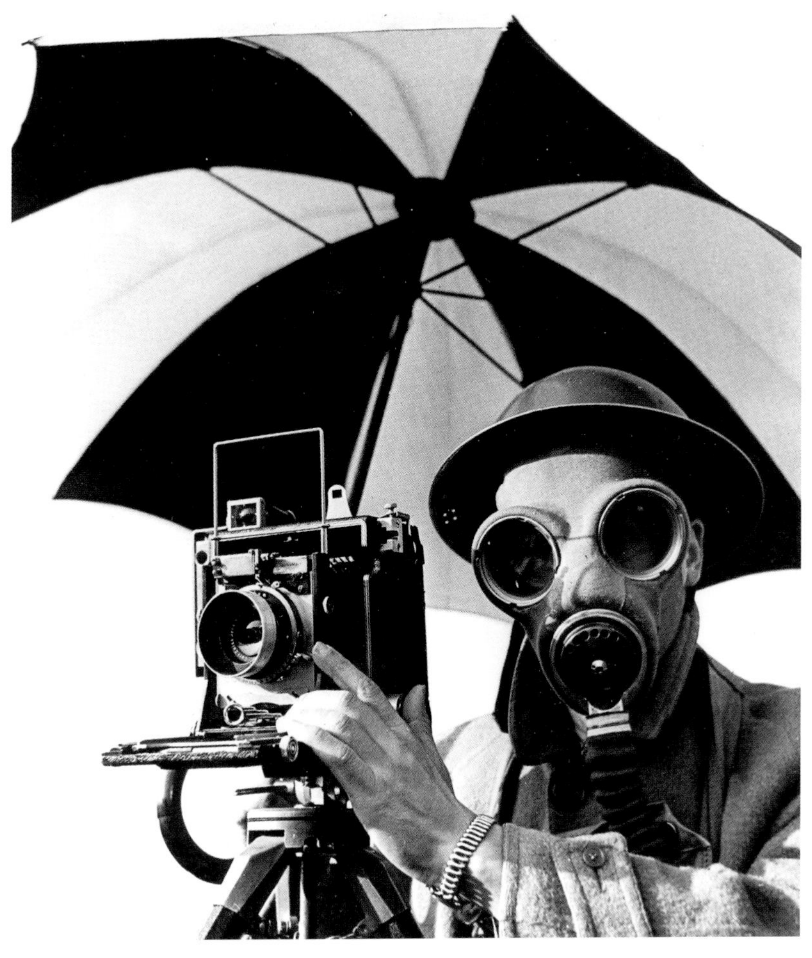

Lee Miller, *David E. Scherman, Dressed for War*, 1942, gelatin silver print, 25.1 × 20.3 cm

IRVING PENN

Truman Capote (1 of 4), New York, 1948

Cornered man is forced to bare his soul

When 23-year-old Truman Capote had his photograph taken by Irving Penn, an established staff photographer at *Vogue*, the author was a boy wonder. But this is no swagger portrait celebrating success: it is more reminiscent of the tortured contortions found in Egon Schiele's paintings. It is also a proto-punk image of contrariness. This image is from Penn's 1947–48 series *Corner Portraits*, in which he explored how famous subjects respond to constraints. Within a narrow receding corner constructed from two studio backdrops and a piece of used carpet, Penn unconventionally allowed his subjects to choose their pose themselves. 'This confinement surprisingly seemed to comfort people, soothing them,' he observed in his 1991 book, *Passage: A Work Record*. Here there is a hint of a trapped animal, kneeling on a chair as though trying to shelter from a rising flood. There is even, with Capote rigidly pushing his fists into his coat, a suggestion of the padded cell and straitjacket. As such, there is something profoundly sympathetic and rather romantic about this psychological portrait of a tortured hero.

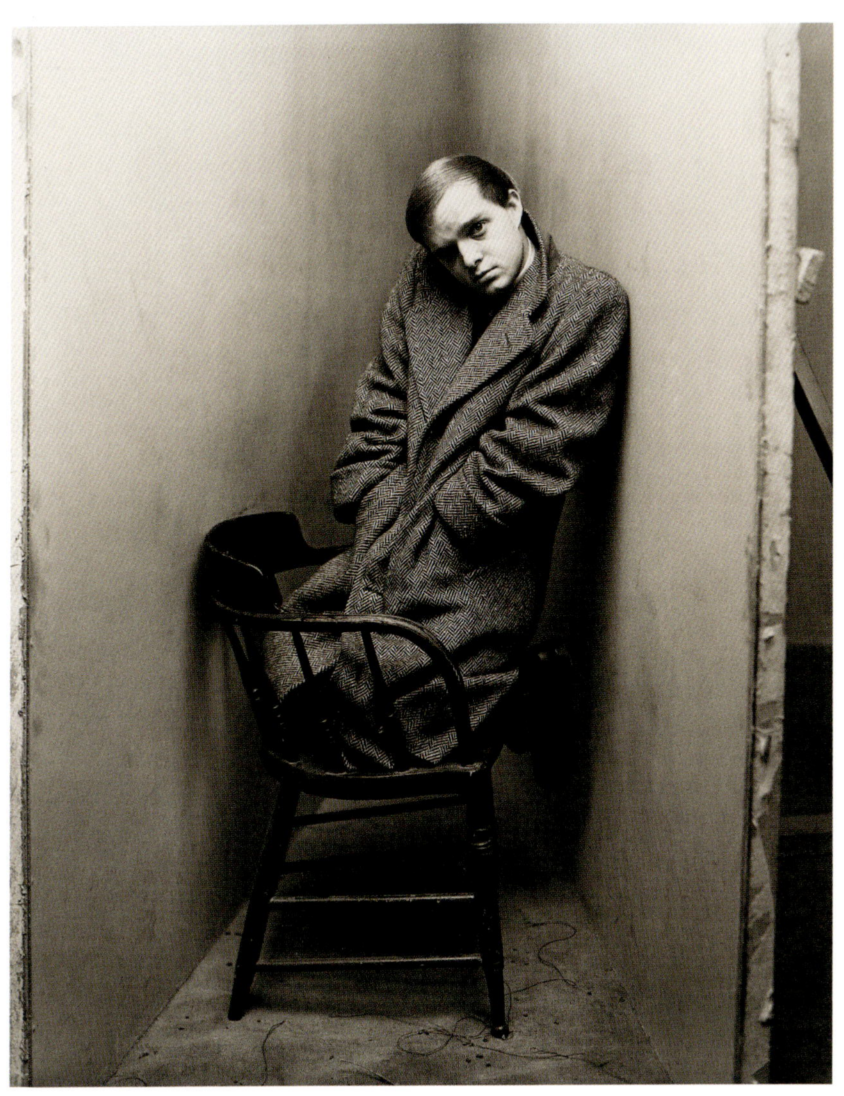

Irving Penn, *Truman Capote (1 of 4), New York*, 1948, gelatin silver print, 24.3 × 19.5 cm

ANDREAS FEININGER

Lunch Hour on Fifth Avenue, 1949

A crowd doesn't have to be faceless

'The world is full of things that the eye doesn't see,' said Andreas Feininger. 'The camera can see more, and sometimes ten times better.' Training first as an architect at the Bauhaus and later in Paris with Le Corbusier, Feininger retained in his photographic work an interest in structure and composition. This stunningly detailed overview of Fifth Avenue in New York is one of Feininger's 'telephotographs', taken with a telephoto lens of his own design which enabled exceptional comprehensiveness and depth of field. Imagine being down in the crowd and taking a picture: you would capture a few people in distorted close-up and beyond that an amorphous mass. By moving further away to see the full scale of the scene – the colossal flow of people going in two directions alongside the flow of traffic – and heightening the verticality of a vertical city, Feininger, who was not particularly interested in individual portraiture, displays his detached and analytical approach. But he also knew just when and where to catch the light. All is bathed in sunshine, the profusion of flags and awnings adding to the celebratory air. And so, far from being cold, the image is full of exuberance.

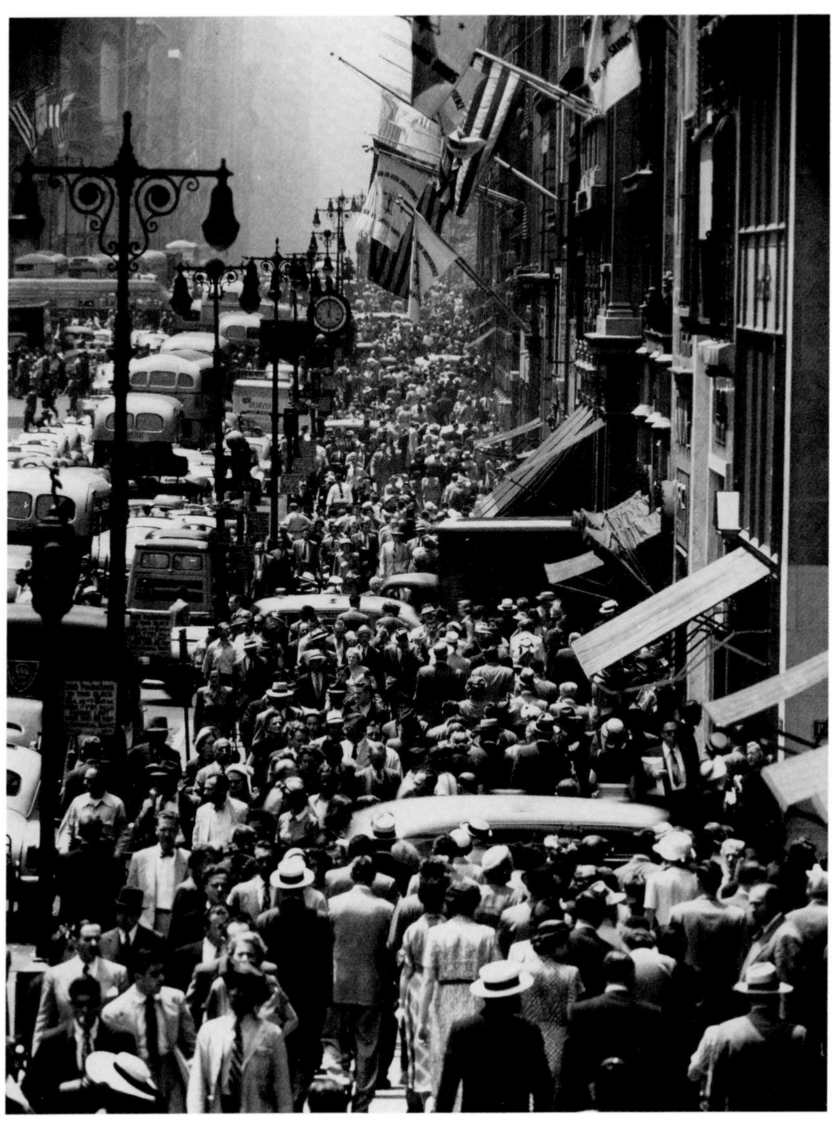

Andreas Feininger, *Lunch Hour on Fifth Avenue*, 1949, gelatin silver print, 48.7 × 39.3 cm

VIVIAN MAIER

Untitled, c.1950s

The Mary Poppins of street photography

'A photograph is a secret about a secret,' Vivian Maier said. 'The more it tells you, the less you know.' This image is a case in point. The woman in it – Maier herself – is a bit of a star, but she was only 'discovered' and acknowledged as a major talent in 2009, almost two years after her death in destitution. For most of her life, she worked as a nanny and caregiver, 'a real, live Mary Poppins,' as one of the children she nannied described her. But in her free time she photographed street life in New York and Chicago, amassing a vast body of work which she kept private. She left behind more than 100,000 images, as well as audio tapes, Super 8 home movie footage and boxes of memorabilia. In her employers' home, Maier had her own bathroom, which she used as her darkroom. But she was more interested in exploring the cityscape and taking pictures than in the process of printing. Using a Rolleiflex camera operated at chest level, so that she could keep eye contact with the person she was photographing, she liked to shoot people on the margins of society. This includes her self-portraits: as a woman in domestic service, she felt herself a shadowy outsider, an enigmatic observer from the edge.

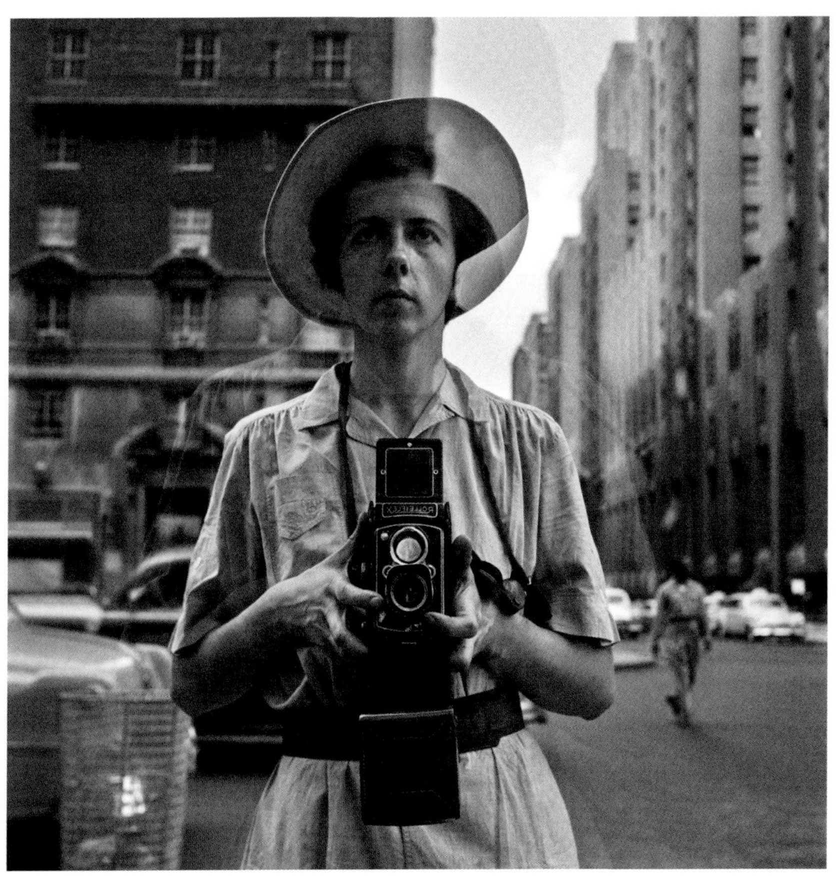

Vivian Maier, *Untitled*, undated, c.1950s

WILLIAM KLEIN

Gun 1, New York, 1954

Photographer's shot is serious child's play

When he returned home after spending eight years abroad, having joined the army at the close of World War II, William Klein was commissioned by *Vogue* to create a book of photos of New York. He found the city changed; possibly he too had changed in his time away. The photos he produced were a brutal, grimy, blurry, high-contrast sea of faces, what he called 'a tabloid gone berserk'. *Vogue* turned them down, finding that they offered too unflattering a portrait of the city, and the resulting book, *Life Is Good & Good For You in New York: Trance Witness Revels* (1956), was published in Paris instead. Klein is no unassuming observer; he is an avid, confrontational, caustic spectator engaging with his subject matter. The expressive violence of the shot was staged: Klein recalled prompting the boy to point the gun at him and 'look tough'. 'He did, and then we both laughed.' And yet the image of the two urchins, one of them mimicking the gangsters of the movies, captures the febrile energy of the street, perhaps also some of the pent-up energy Klein brought back from his time in the military. He saw the image of the two boys, one tough, the other gentle, as 'a double self-portrait'.

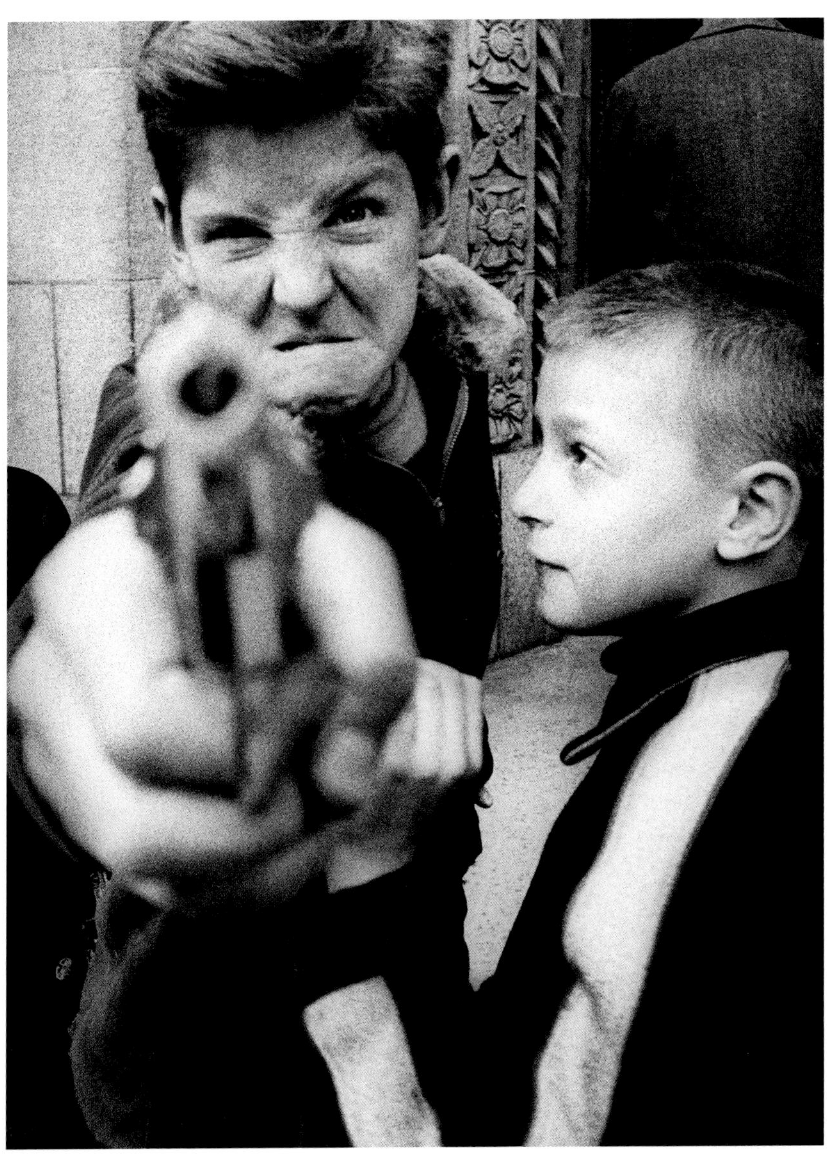

William Klein, *Gun 1, New York*, 1954, gelatin silver print, 45.4 × 33.3 cm, Metropolitan Museum of Art, New York

ROBERT FRANK

Trolley – New Orleans, 1955

The book that revolutionised America's self-image

This profoundly unsettling photograph of a racially segregated tram in 1955 New Orleans was chosen by its author Robert Frank for the cover of his uniquely influential book *The Americans* (1959). The Swiss-born Frank had come to America intending to document the 'land of the free'. In 1955–56 he travelled by car from New York to California, and photographed parades, drugstores, street crowds, luncheonettes and American flags in rough, sometimes blurred compositions, revealing a fallen world deeply at odds with the American Dream. He focused especially on the realities of the Black experience. *Trolley – New Orleans* is an image of division and exile. It's also a portrait gallery, with Black and white passengers, with their varying expressions, framed by stark vertical prison-like bars. The swirling reflections in the upper windows remind us that the tram is travelling: Frank caught this eloquent composition on the fly. The little girl's hand rests on the 'race screen', the wooden separator that could be moved backwards if more white passengers got on the trolley. In fact, segregation was at breaking point in 1955: in nearby Alabama, a few weeks after *Trolley – New Orleans* was taken, Black Civil Rights activist Rosa Parks refused to go to the back of the bus.

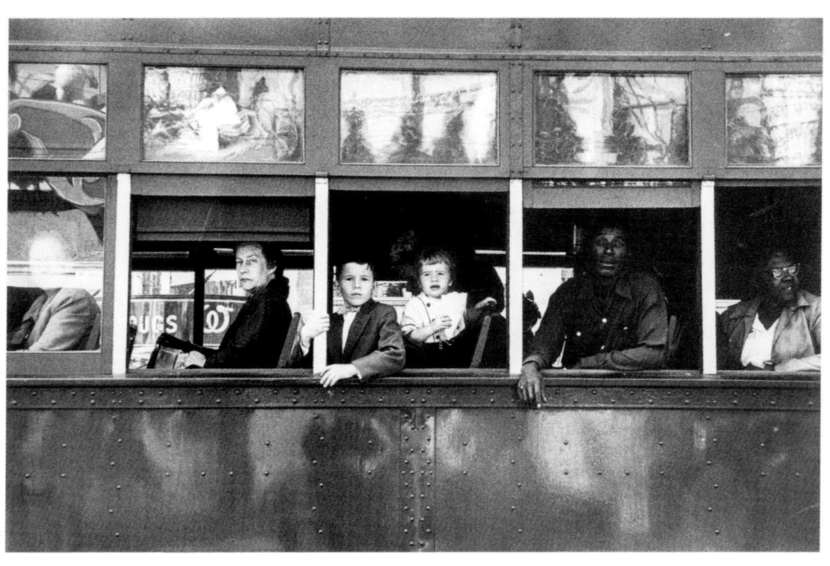

Robert Frank, *Trolley – New Orleans*, 1955, gelatin silver print, 23.1 × 34 cm, The Museum of Modern Art, New York

GRACE ROBERTSON

On the Caterpillar, Women's Pub Outing, 1956

Motion and emotion: women seize the day

As one of very few female photojournalists in the 1950s, Grace Robertson often turned her lens in the direction of women subjects. One such (repeated) assignment was to follow a group of women who frequented the same pub and once a year went on a day out together, packing sandwiches and beer and wearing their best frocks. 'This story was very human,' Robertson said. 'It cut across the class system.' What is so joyous about this image is its rippling, dynamic quality: as the Caterpillar undulates and accelerates, the demeanour of the women changes from the distracted seriousness of the back row through to a more relaxed, slightly vacant-looking pair; then to two women who are smiling, perhaps in anticipation of the swell; and finally to the women in the front row who are laughing, skirts billowing, revealing decorous bloomers. The image is partly a tribute to a 1949 photograph by Kurt Hutton of pretty young women on a fairground ride with their skirts flying up. But what Robertson captures is a group of ordinary, middle-aged women from a close-knit community enjoying a rare moment of leisure away from their domestic responsibilities.

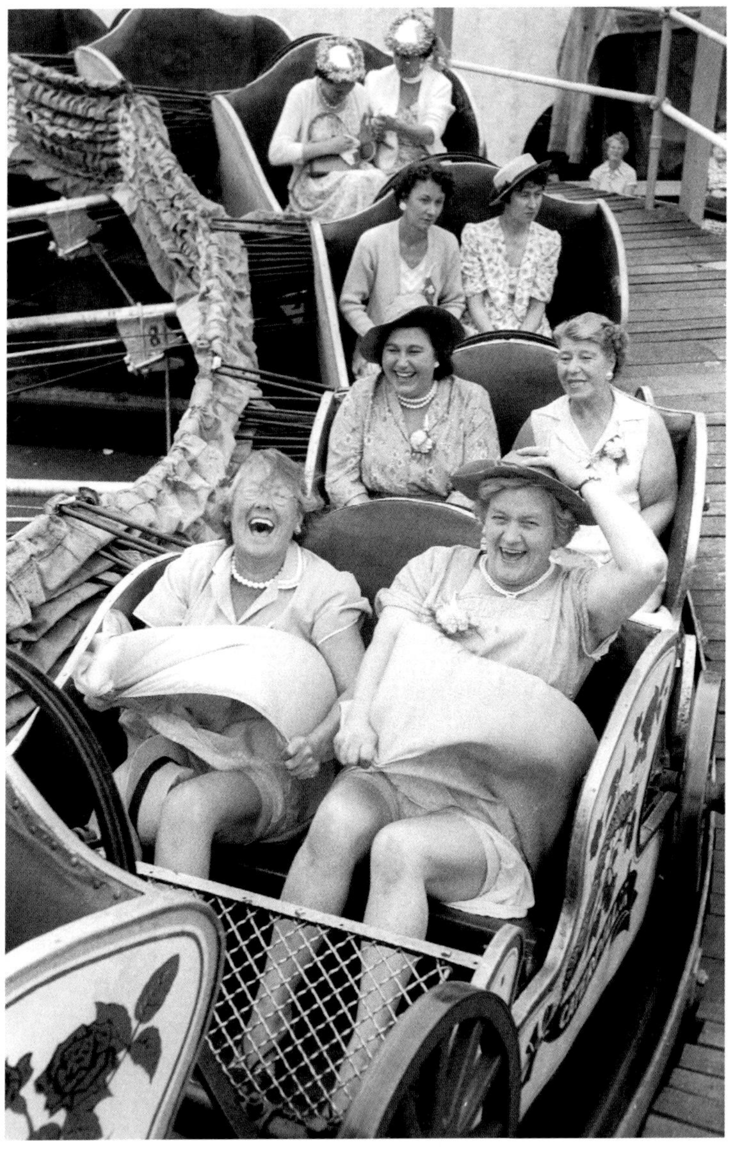

Grace Robertson, *On the Caterpillar, Women's Pub Outing*, 1956, gelatin silver print, 50.5 × 40.5 cm

SAUL LEITER

Cap, c.1960

Through a glass, darkly

It's like being a child again, in the back seat of a car, staring in wonder for the first time at the play of condensation on the window and, through it, at the distortions of light and colour beyond. As an artist, Abstract Expressionist painter turned self-taught street photographer Saul Leiter believed in bringing 'mishmoshy confusion into order'. Many of his subjects are reflected in or seen through windows. He got under the skin of New York street life, capturing it in compositions often verging on abstraction. Leiter used out-of-date Kodachrome film which gave his pictures a more muted quality, eschewing sharpness. Here, alongside a dark shape, we see the blurred silhouette of a passer-by wearing a cap, the partially faded signage printed on a shop window constellated with rain drops. Meagre winter light is cast over bitter greys and blacks. In the background, there is a streak of warm yellow – a passing taxi or truck, we can't be sure. That yellow is important: Leiter was a pioneer of colour photography as fine art rather than a gimmick. Here are transience and mystery: life in reflection.

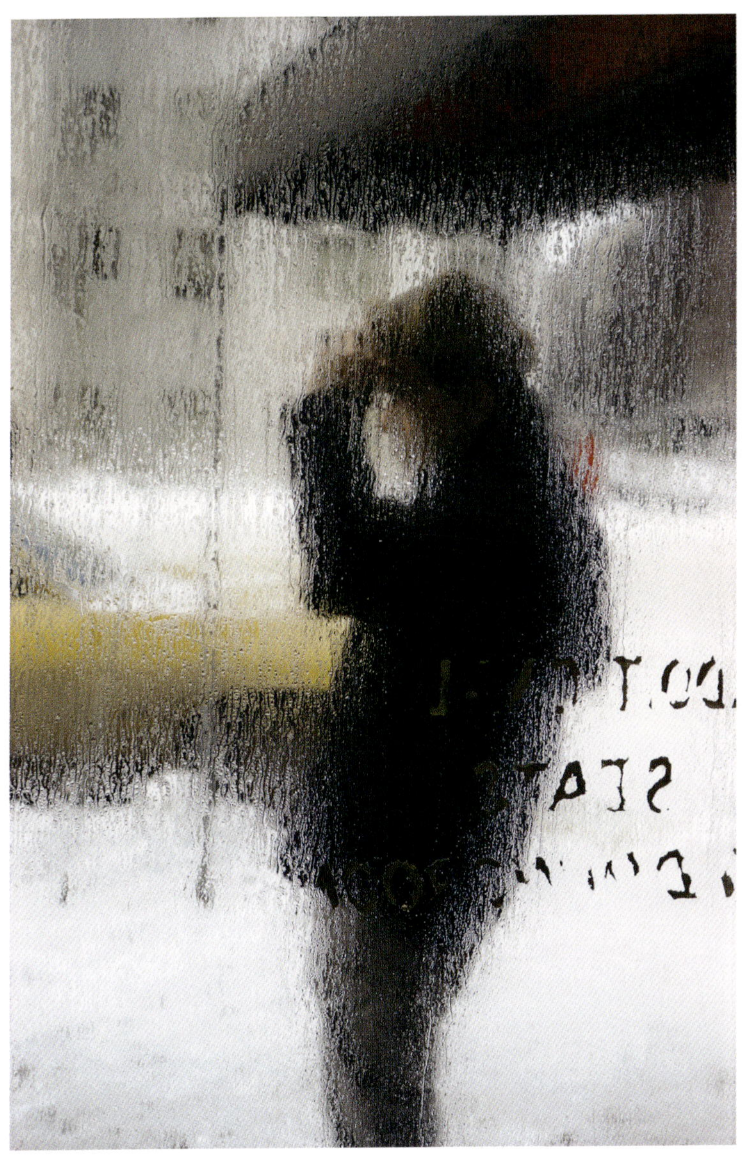

Saul Leiter, *Cap*, c.1960

EVE ARNOLD

Malcolm X, Chicago, 1962

Sitter delivers mystique-shaping masterclass

In the early 1960s, *Life* magazine sent photojournalist Eve Arnold to shadow the Nation of Islam at their meetings and rallies. During that time Arnold profiled Malcolm X, a Muslim minister and vocal advocate for Black empowerment in the Civil Rights movement. As with Arnold's portraits of Marilyn Monroe taken on the set of *The Misfits*, there is a behind-the-scenes quality to the pictures, but with one significant difference: Malcolm X, a shrewd visual strategist focused on crafting his own persona, took a decisive lead in the process. 'Malcolm set up the shots and I clicked the camera. It was hilarious,' Arnold said of the experience. In this iconic image, in which he sports a sharp black suit and tilted fedora, his outfit completed with an Islamic ring adorned with a star and a crescent moon, he looks very put together, his styling almost dandyish. At the same time, he is photographed in profile in the manner of a king or emperor stamped on a coin – a politically resonant and artfully staged emblem of power.

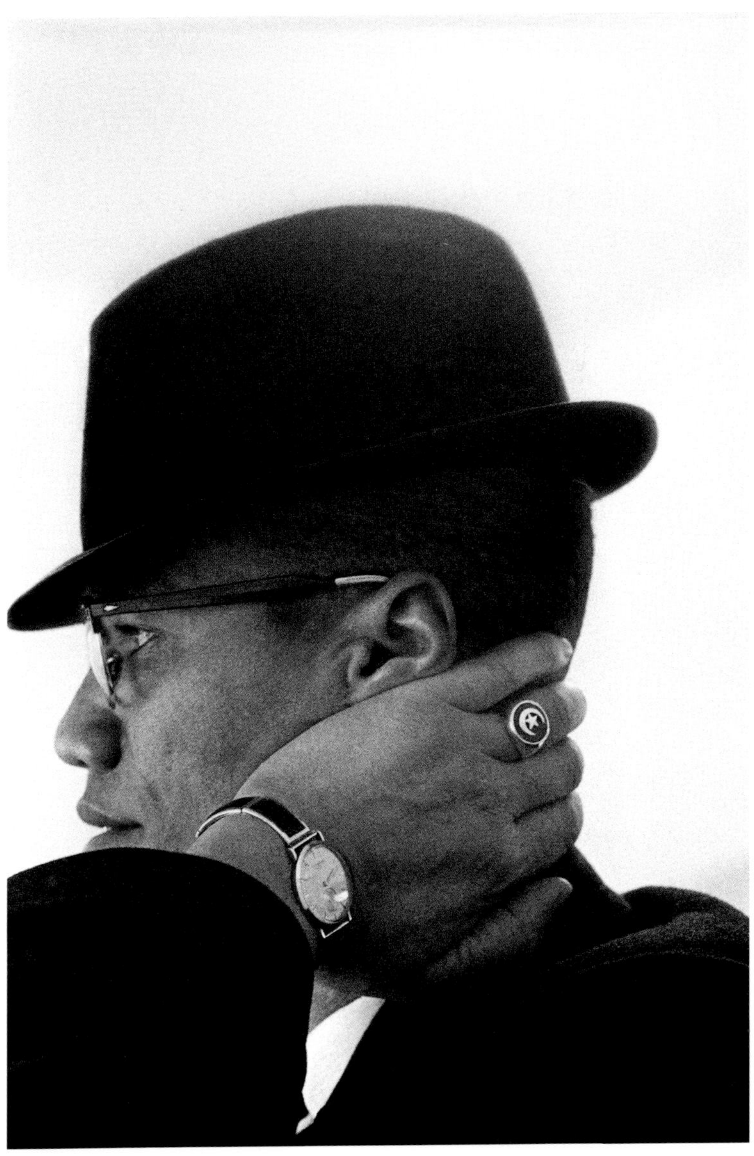

Eve Arnold, *Malcolm X during his visit to enterprises owned by black muslims, Chicago*, 1962, silver gelatin print

MALICK SIDIBÉ

Nuit de Noël (Happy Club), 1963

Dancing out of colonialism and into freedom

Christmas Eve, 1963, in Bamako, Mali: it's warm and the party is happening outside, with a small record player providing the soundtrack, which is likely to be rhythm and blues, rock'n'roll – perhaps even the twist. In 1960, Mali had gained independence from France, and what Malick Sidibé – who in those days went from one party to the next on his bicycle – captures here is the sense of liberation, optimism and youthful energy that followed. Young people like this brother and sister, here teaching each other some dance steps, threw themselves into the joys of music, late-night partying and drinking. There was a sense that, like the country's dancing youth, society was also in motion, crossing over into a new era. But from the mid-1960s, such exuberant freedom would be cut short by increasingly repressive political regimes. Curfews were imposed and parties went underground. 'For me,' Sidibé said, 'photography is all about youth.' And with this image he has captured an iconic moment of playful intimacy in which two dapper siblings, their bodies framed by curving trees, are moving against the conventions of their parents' generation.

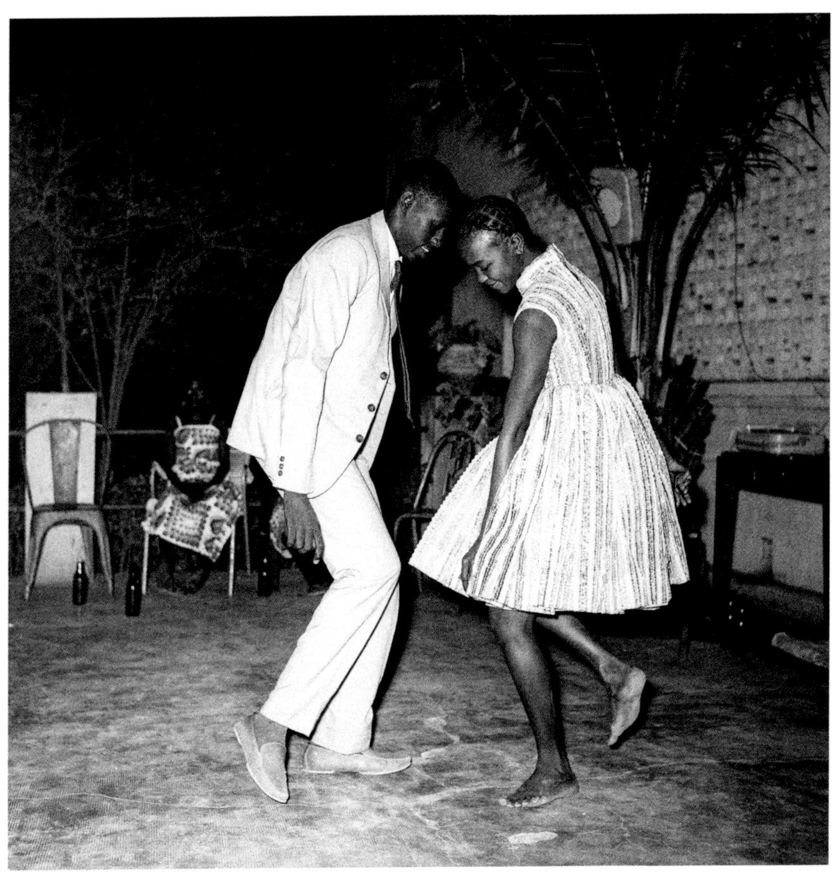

Malick Sidibé, *Nuit de Noël (Happy Club)*, 1963,
gelatin silver print, 33.3 × 34 cm, Museum of Modern Art, New York

GARRY WINOGRAND

New York, 1965

The street turns paranoid as the Sixties begin to sour

An eye-catching passer-by on a city street: it's a familiar motif in art, but in Garry Winogrand's image an ominous shadow hangs over the scene. Winogrand worked at a headlong rate, as though attempting to record all of life. He produced 20,000 rolls of film and was more interested in taking pictures than in printing them: much of his work was only developed after he died at the age of 56. He shot the streets of New York compulsively in the 1960s, a time of social and political unrest, photographing politicians, soldiers, hippies and anti-war protesters, absorbing the era's air of anxiety. While some street photographers work unobtrusively, Winogrand's style is more confrontational: he likes to push right in. Here, it feels like the photographer is shooting from above, towering over the passing woman and getting in her way, as though they are on a collision course and she is about to walk into him. Perhaps this is why she will not look at the camera, staring straight ahead and striding past, holding on tightly to her bags. Behind her, two men in suits are smiling. If this were a still from a Cold War thriller, they might be shadowing her.

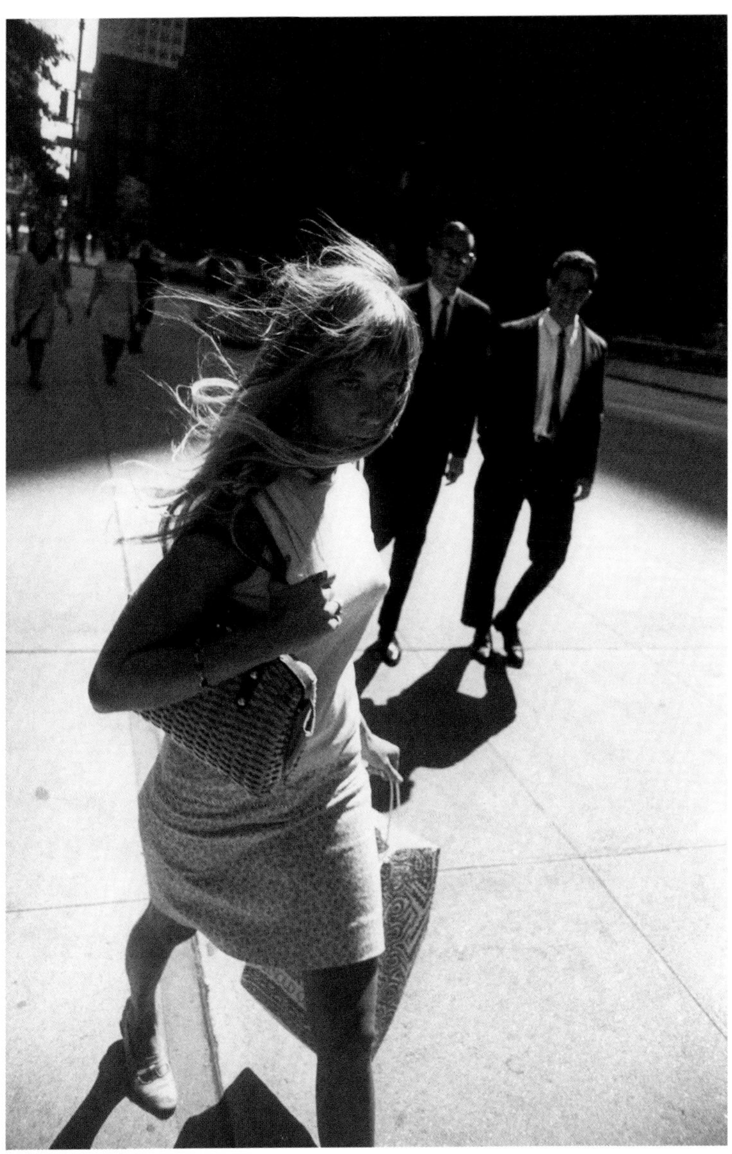

Garry Winogrand, *New York*, 1965, gelatin silver print, 33 × 22cm

WILLIAM EGGLESTON

Untitled (Greenwood, Mississippi), 1973

A democratic way of looking around

What do you see when you're lying in bed looking at the ceiling? In this image, the sight of a shabby ceiling is made riveting by its ultra-vivid colour: the brilliant lipstick-red of blood and passion, diagonally divided by white electric wires connected to a naked lightbulb. We're looking at a formal composition verging on abstraction. William Eggleston's subject matter is everyday life in the southern states of America, where he has photographed people, cars, petrol stations and interiors. In 1976, he was the first photographer to be given a solo exhibition of colour work at MoMA in New York – up to this point artist (as opposed to commercial or amateur) photographers worked almost exclusively in black and white. Eggleston's turning to colour wasn't so much a professional decision as an expression of desire: 'I wanted to see things in colour, because the world was in colour.' His everyday images, captured without making any value judgment, are unforgettable. In 1973, when he made this picture, Eggleston had just discovered dye transfer printing, whose saturated palette was associated with advertising. In this image of a friend's guestroom ceiling, the maximal presence of the colour red – with some cropped Kama Sutra pictures in primary colours adding an extra edge – would have seemed shocking and new, elevating a seedy setting into a mysterious still life.

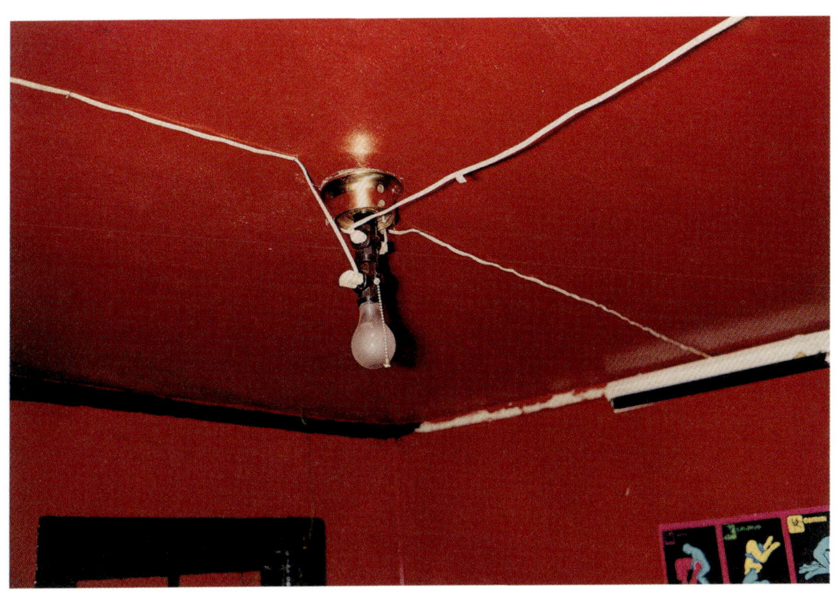

William Eggleston, *Untitled (Greenwod, Mississippi)*, 1973, dye transfer print, 31.3 × 47 cm

JOEL MEYEROWITZ

New York City, West 46th Street, 1976

A new visual 'street jazz' is born

'I wanted to spread the energy that I felt on the street all over the frame,' says American street photographer Joel Meyerowitz. When he took this shot, he was moving from the lucky 'catch' of his pioneering black-and-white pictures – that is, pictures focused on single, central incidents – to the greater range of descriptive content and pulsating emotion made possible by colour, which was becoming easier and cheaper to process. In 1976, Meyerowitz decided to pursue field photographs of urban traffic and chaos and 'go really big' with a wooden 8x10 Deardorff camera and a wide-angle lens. He was ahead of his time and yearned for huge, wall-sized prints when no galleries understood the point of them. This mindset would take 25 years to change. But at any size, this photo is a pinball machine of primary colours and arrows and gazes pointing in all directions. It's thrumming and blaring, verging on synaesthesia – it's *noisy*. Street jazz! 'You just had to get in the same groove,' Meyerowitz knew. Everything is fully present: a swaying belt, a cigar, a mock medieval statue in a niche. In black and white this would be 'nothing', Meyerowitz reflected, but in colour it's 'a moment where the fourth wall gives way and we are there.'

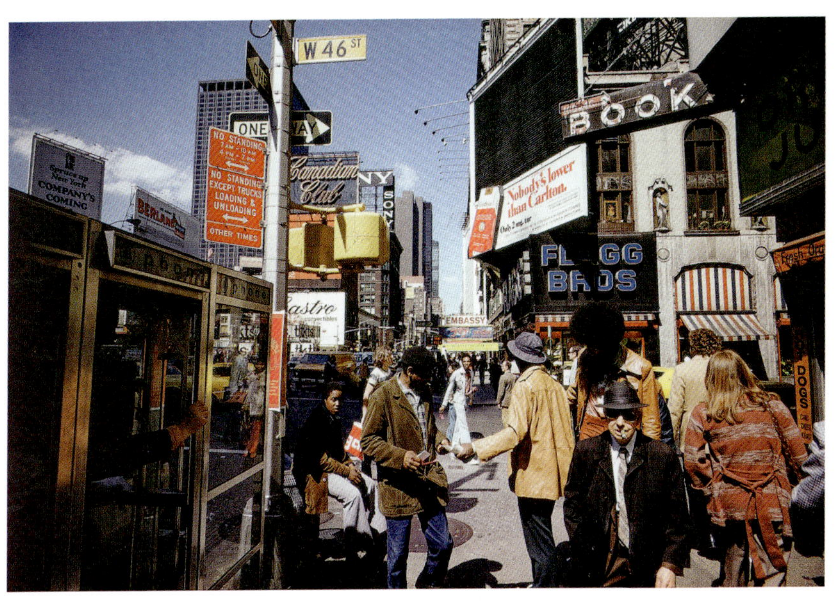

Joel Meyerowitz, *New York City, West 46th Street*, 1976, dye transfer print, 40.3 × 59.1 cm

STEPHEN SHORE

Ginger Shore, West Palm Beach, Florida, 1977

Seventies time capsule and oblique portrait

So much *green*! It signals a different kind of seeing. It's easy to underestimate what a pioneer Stephen Shore was. Colour photography was not considered a valid medium for art photography at the beginning of the 1970s. But in contrast with 'decisive moments' elevated by black-and-white to the status of works of art, Shore wanted 'pictures that felt as natural as speaking'. This meant colour, and a resolutely non-glossy recording of a road trip across America, exploring ordinary sights such as food on a diner table, trucks, petrol stations and motel rooms. These shots were extraordinarily influential, establishing a new and highly cinematic imagery of Americana. This unassuming photograph of his wife, which might have been snapped mid-conversation, also has a painterly air. The feel is casual, unforced. At the same time, colour creates mood, the lines of the open car doors suggesting a dynamic sense of freedom and adventure. Ginger Shore has turned away, and this creates a great desire to see the face of this mysterious person, the heroine of Shore's freewheeling road movie.

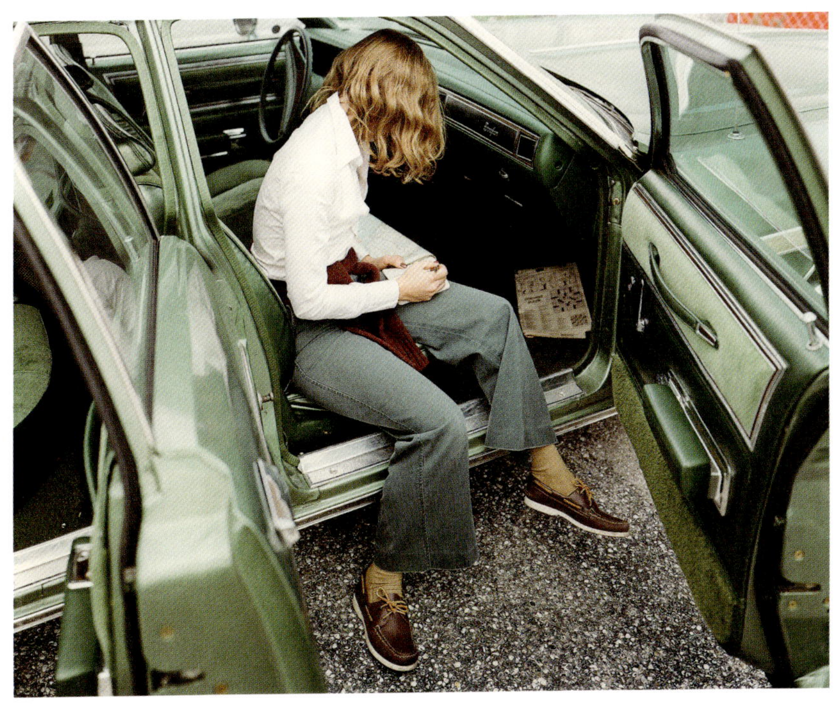

Stephen Shore, *Ginger Shore, West Palm Beach, Florida*, 1977

GUY BOURDIN

Untitled, 1978

Swimwear photo turns into staged psychodrama

Blue was never quite blue enough for Guy Bourdin, who during a shoot by the ocean had his assistants throw bucket after bucket of dye into the waves to make them more vivid – all in vain as the dye kept washing away. No such problem here, where the empty swimming pool is painted an electrifying shade. Influenced by his mentor Man Ray (p.32), the Surrealist paintings of René Magritte and the films of Luis Buñuel, Bourdin was always intent on highlighting the artifice of his fashion photographs. What seduces us in his work isn't fashion itself, but the image of fashion that he conjures up. Bourdin relished total creative control and was famous for submitting a single cropped transparency for publication, rather than whole sheets of options for the art editor to consider. This unsettling mise-en-scène is typical of his taste for sexually charged drama, mystery and danger. Here, the model, in trademark Bourdin doll-like make-up, is braced as tightly as a bow and arrow, seemingly about to launch herself backwards – onto brightly painted concrete. Now we are in suspense! Yes, she is looking at us defiantly, signalling that this is only make-believe, but that doesn't quite dispel the edgy unease produced by the image. There is nothing escapist about this off-kilter fashion tableau.

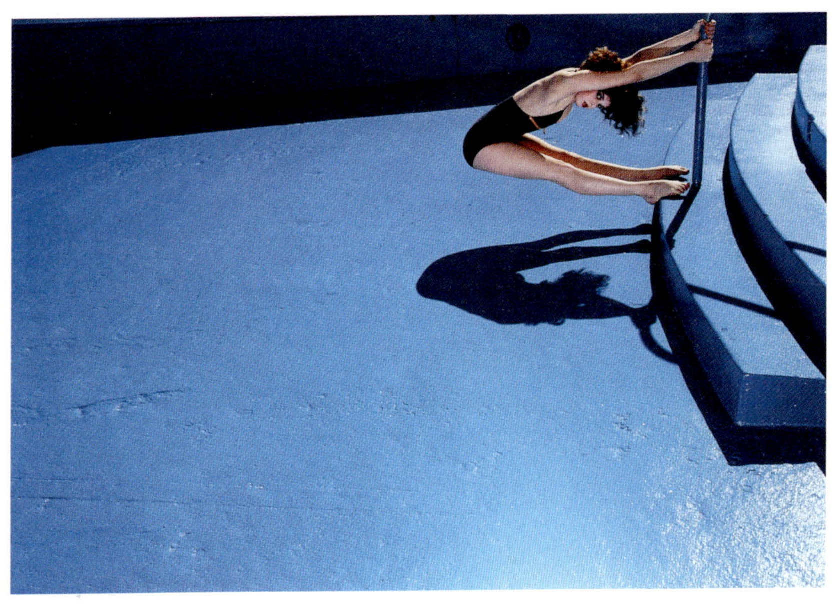

Guy Bourdin, *Untitled*, 1978

HELMUT NEWTON

Self-Portrait with Wife and Models, 1981

'Kink king' goes through the looking glass

'If a photographer says he is not a voyeur, he is an idiot,' declared German photographer Helmut Newton, also known as the 'king of kink'. Here we too are placed in the position of a voyeur looking, as if through a peephole, at Newton, the subject of this self-portrait. Behind the mask of his camera, he almost disappears from view, radically upstaged by the women in the shot. Daytime Paris is visible through the open window, and yet a nocturnal film noir atmosphere permeates the scene. There is a suggestion of obsessively, fetishistically staged debauchery. The women, in their different ways, exude confidence and power: the Amazonian model in her high heels, striking a pose somewhere between classical statuary and stage burlesque; Newton's wife June (also known as Alice Springs and herself a photographer) impassively watching the scene. This is Helmut Newton's sweet spot: to produce transgressive, highly erotic images that – often to the marked displeasure of his brand-conscious fashion clients – bring the models' sexuality into triumphant focus.

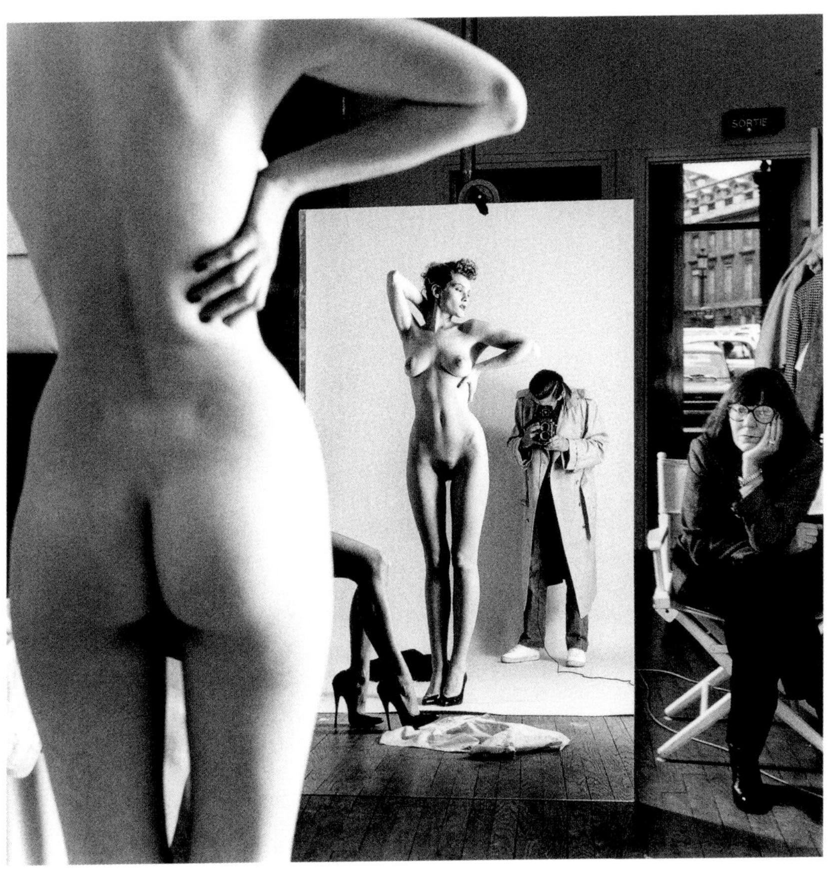

Helmut Newton, *Self-Portrait with Wife and Models*,
Vogue Studios, Paris, 1981, gelatin silver print, 118.1 × 121 cm

CINDY SHERMAN

Untitled #92, 1981

Something wicked this way comes; artist isn't quite herself

Photography meets performance art in this arresting image. In her meticulously staged works, where she appears as a series of different fictional characters – bored housewife, jilted mistress, jaded seductress – American artist Cindy Sherman unpicks the effects exerted on the construction of individual identity by mass-media imagery. This photograph shows Sherman in character as a young girl in peril, crouching on the floor, her expression full of anguish as she looks up at an unseen person – a possible attacker? Her hair is wet: has she been running in film noir rain? Appropriating conventions from Alfred Hitchcock films of the 1950s and 60s, most notably the performances of Tippi Hedren in *The Birds* and Janet Leigh in *Psycho*, the image reads like a still taken from an imaginary movie of which Sherman is the star. Part of a series that propelled Sherman's career entitled *Centerfolds*, Sherman is here reclaiming the sexualised Playboy playmate format where women's bodies are displayed for the enjoyment of the masculine gaze. Being in control as both the subject and the maker of her image, she points out the artificial construction of female stereotypes and defeats expectations of titillation with something unsettling instead.

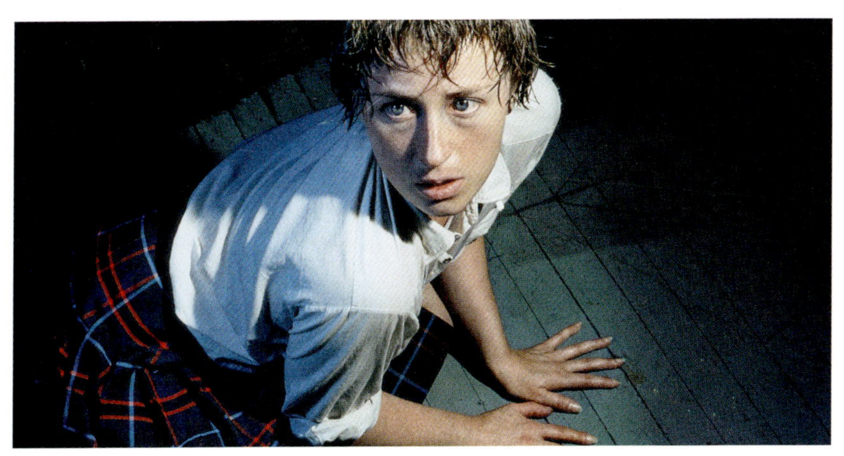

Cindy Sherman, *Untitled* #92, 1981

STEVE MCCURRY

Afghan Girl, 1984

'Afghan Mona Lisa' becomes symbol of war's human cost

American photojournalist Steve McCurry took this arresting portrait of a 12-year-old Pashtun girl in a makeshift school tent at the Nasir Bhag refugee camp in Pakistan during the Soviet invasion of Afghanistan. He captured a fleeting expression. For just two frames she makes direct eye contact with McCurry, an intense look on her face; 'and then it was gone,' he recalled, and the child rejoined her friends. Initially, the picture editor of *National Geographic* magazine thought the image 'too disturbing' for its cover, but the editor-in-chief disagreed and it appeared on the front of the June 1985 issue. With its intense colour play of vivid green and red, its focus on the child's challenging gaze and its startling mix of beauty and pathos, the image immediately became iconic. Despite being one of the most recognised photographs in the world, the identity of the anonymous subject (sometimes compared to the Mona Lisa for her similarly mysterious quality) was not recorded in the original article. In 2002, after years of searching, McCurry and the *National Geographic* team located her; Sharbat Gula, now married with children, had no idea that she was the face of victims of war, a symbol of the plight of displaced refugees.

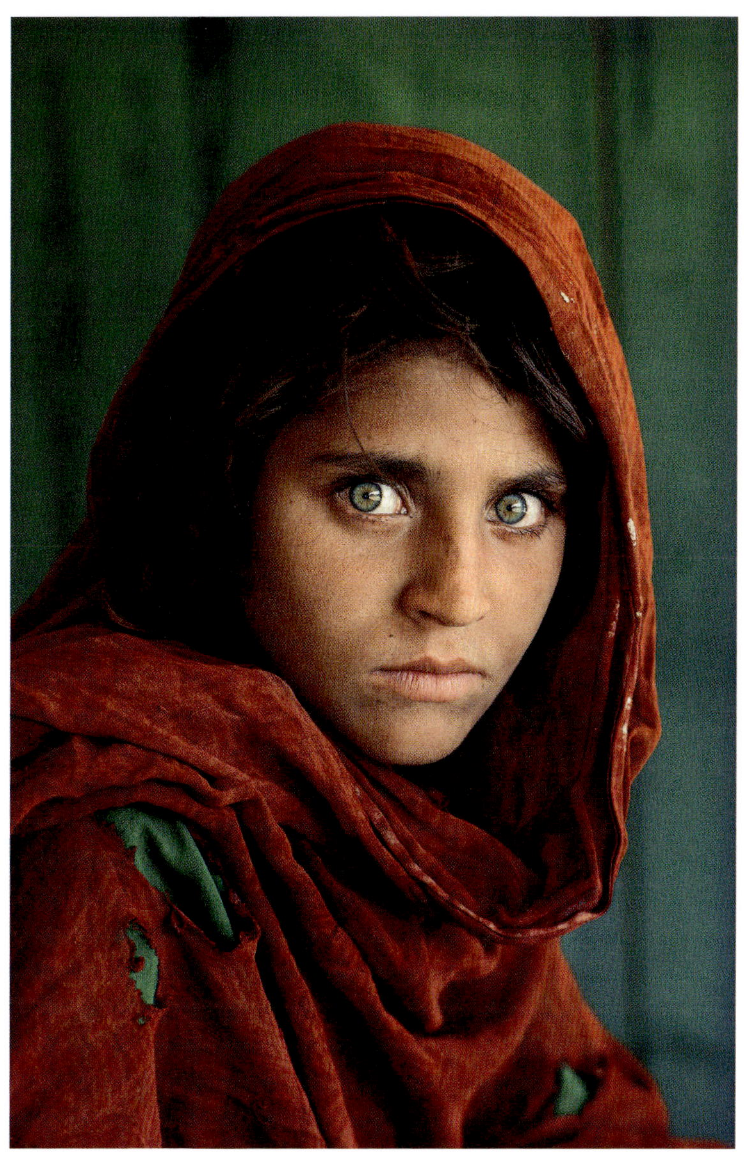

Steve McCurry, *Afghan Girl*, 1984

LARRY SULTAN

Practicing Golf Swing, 1986

Revering the family; revising the American Dream

What are family home movies? Partly, they are documents of family life, but they are also, as Larry Sultan discovered when re-watching those made in his childhood, projected dreams of family life, 'like a good folk tale'. In the conceptual series *Pictures from Home* (1983–92) – a narrative collage of Sultan's own photographs of his ageing parents mixed with snapshots and home-movie stills – the photographer wanted, against the background of the Reagan era and of his difficult relationship with his father, to expose the dangers of growing up with images of success and the American Dream. As Sultan enlisted his parents' collaboration to appear in staged photographs in their home in Los Angeles, the images also became about the ability of photography to stop time, making his parents immortal. Here, Sultan's retiree father is practising his golf swing in the iconic pose of a tournament trophy, but the frailty of his bare legs reveals his age. The image sits somewhere between documentary and performance, just as, ever so slightly surreally, Sultan's father is practising indoors on a green deep-pile carpet that looks like turf, while we glimpse the outdoors through the sunlit drapes.

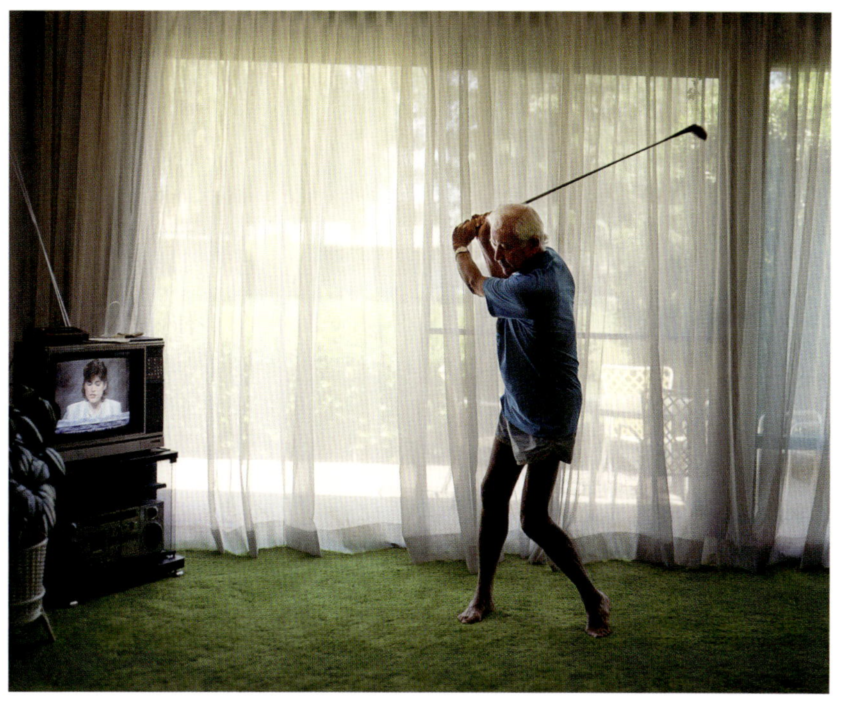

Larry Sultan, *Practicing Golf Swing*, 1986, from the series *Pictures from Home*

DAVID HOCKNEY

Pearblossom Highway, 1986

Road movie as photomontage reveals nature of perception

'You can see the cracks in the enamel,' British photographer and artist David Hockney said of this 'joiner', a choppy collage representation of a road trip through the desert, made up of 650 photographs taken over nine days and arranged into a single whole image. The result, where the edges of all photographs are visible, is a complex, impressionistic, somewhat Cubist account of a road trip as it is experienced in the mind, looking down and up and in every direction. Hockney explained that it combines the two different perspectives of the driver looking at road signs and the passenger who is looking all around, noticing litter, shrubs, Joshua trees and the edges where desert meets tarmac. Hockney is also a painter, and the most painterly part of the picture is the sky which, with its mosaic of blues, looks like a swimming pool – one that Hockney might have indeed painted. 'I constructed my picture with pictures of surfaces,' he said, 'and the "space" then is made in the mind, perhaps the only place it actually exists.'

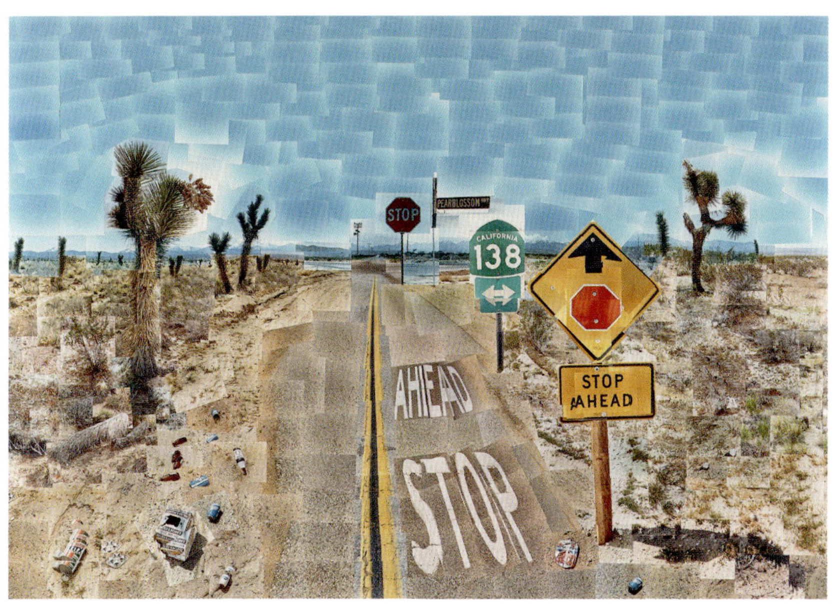

David Hockney, *Pearblossom Hwy., 11-18th April 1986* (Second Version)
photographic collage, 181.6 × 271.8 cm

DAIDO MORIYAMA

Tights in Shimotakaido, 1986

Extreme close-up reveals hidden world

'In any black and white image there is some variety of eroticism,' Daido Moriyama has stated enigmatically. This image is a case in point: an extreme close-up of a woman's legs encased in fishnet tights that is openly erotic, even fetishistic. And the image is one of many obsessive variations on the same theme in Moriyama's 1980s series *How to Create a Beautiful Picture 6: Tights in Shimotakaido*. But there is more going on here: Moriyama gets close enough to his subject for reality to become fragmented, transformed into something unfamiliar, an imaginary landscape. The photographer often compares his point of view to the inquisitive gaze of a wandering dog (and has indeed said that the first photographs he took were of his family dog). There is certainly a human body in the picture, but at the same time it is a composition consisting of disorientating whorls and meshes. Moriyama's lens provides, in his own words, 'a unique way of encountering genuine reality'.

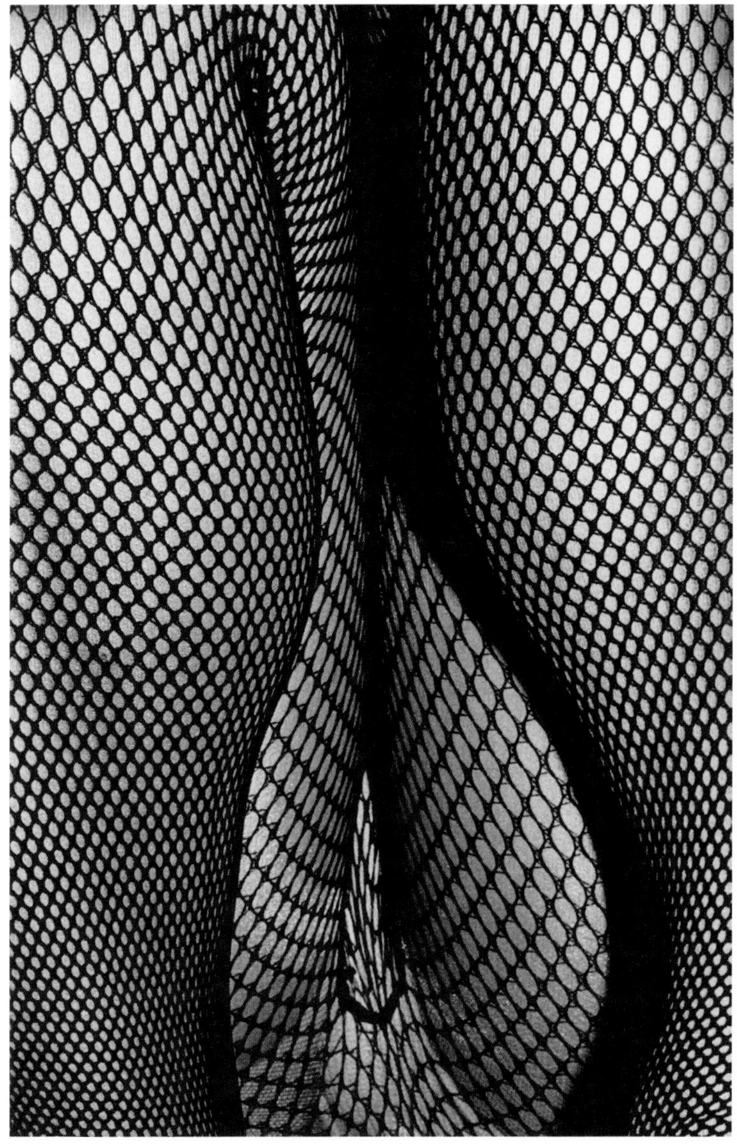

Daido Moriyama, *Tights in Shimotakaido*, 1986, gelatin silver print, 41.2 × 27.5 cm

HELEN LEVITT

New York City (Phone Booth), 1988

Room for one more? The street as playground

To Helen Levitt, the street was 'above all, a theatre and a battleground'. Influenced by Surrealism and silent film, she aimed to capture the poetics of everyday life and showed a particular interest in the body language of children's play. She was drawn to children's anarchic physical presence in the street, their expressive awkwardness, the way they twisted their bodies into shapes. This photo was taken later in Levitt's career, at a time when it was less common to see children playing outside. So when Levitt saw the woman standing in the phone box with her daughter, she waited, and then she caught the boy's comic-heroic attempt to squeeze himself into the booth. The scene is reminiscent of the 1950s 'phone-box stuffing fad', where students tried to fit as many people as possible into a booth, photographing the results. Here, however, the act was unplanned, a 'decisive moment' or, in Levitt's own words, an 'accidental disarrangement' seized upon by the photographer and turned into an intuitive composition. To the left, a deep perspective; to the right, a flattened view blocked by traffic; in the middle, a struggle for space which also suggests the contortions of contemporary dance.

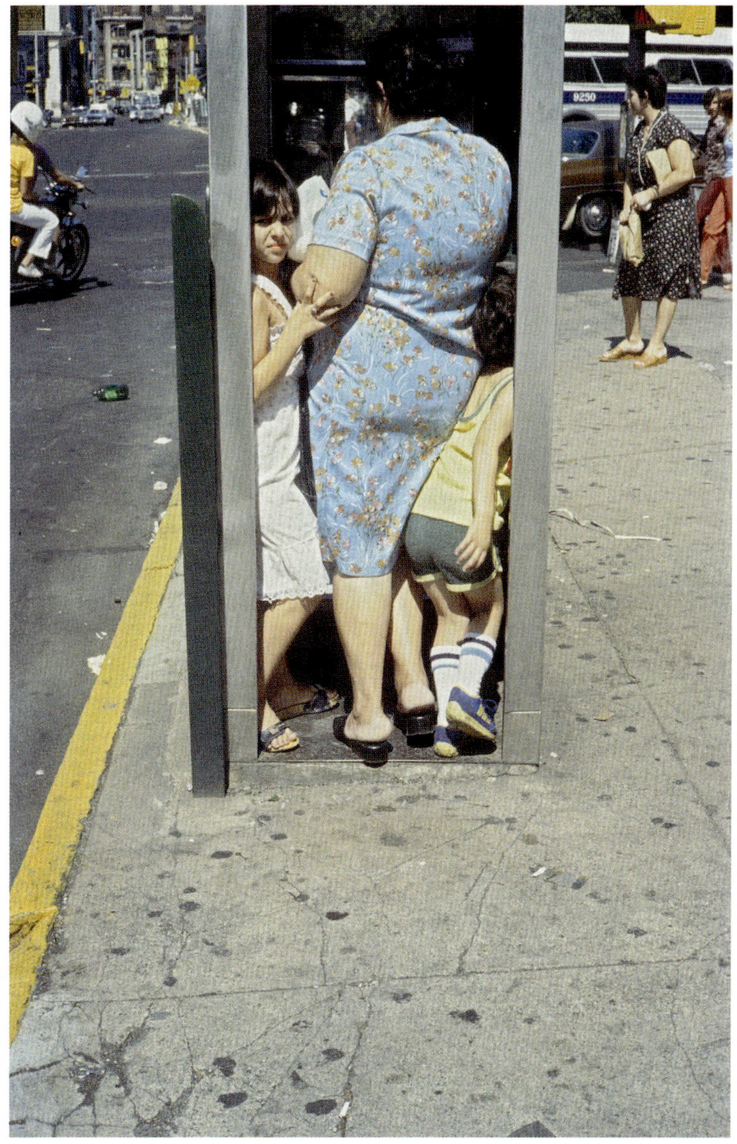

Helen Levitt, *New York City (Phone Booth)*, 1988

ANDREAS STERZING

David Wojnarowicz (Silence = Death), 1989

Portrait of a silenced man becomes icon of political defiance

A photograph may be many things: a witness-bearing historical document; an expression of aesthetic revolt; an act of political protest. This portrait of the New York artist and activist David Wojnarowicz, taken by his friend the German photographer Andreas Sterzing at the height of the AIDS crisis, is all three. Its irresistible persuasive force, both at the time of its making in 1989 and across the following decades, won it a place in the *New York Times Magazine*'s list of the 25 most influential works of American protest art since the Second World War. The first cases of AIDS were recorded in the early 1980s, but it was only in 1987 that President Ronald Reagan finally spoke publicly about the issue. This drawn-out political silence did indeed mean death for many. The titular slogan was popularised by an iconic 1987 poster which carried the verbal equation beneath a pink triangle, but achieved its most direct, visceral expression in Sterzing's still image, created for Rosa von Praunheim and Phil Zwickler's 1990 documentary film *Silence = Death*. Wojnarowicz's mouth may have been stopped, but his unflinching gaze refuses to be denied. Wojnarowicz would die from AIDS-related complications, aged 37, in 1992.

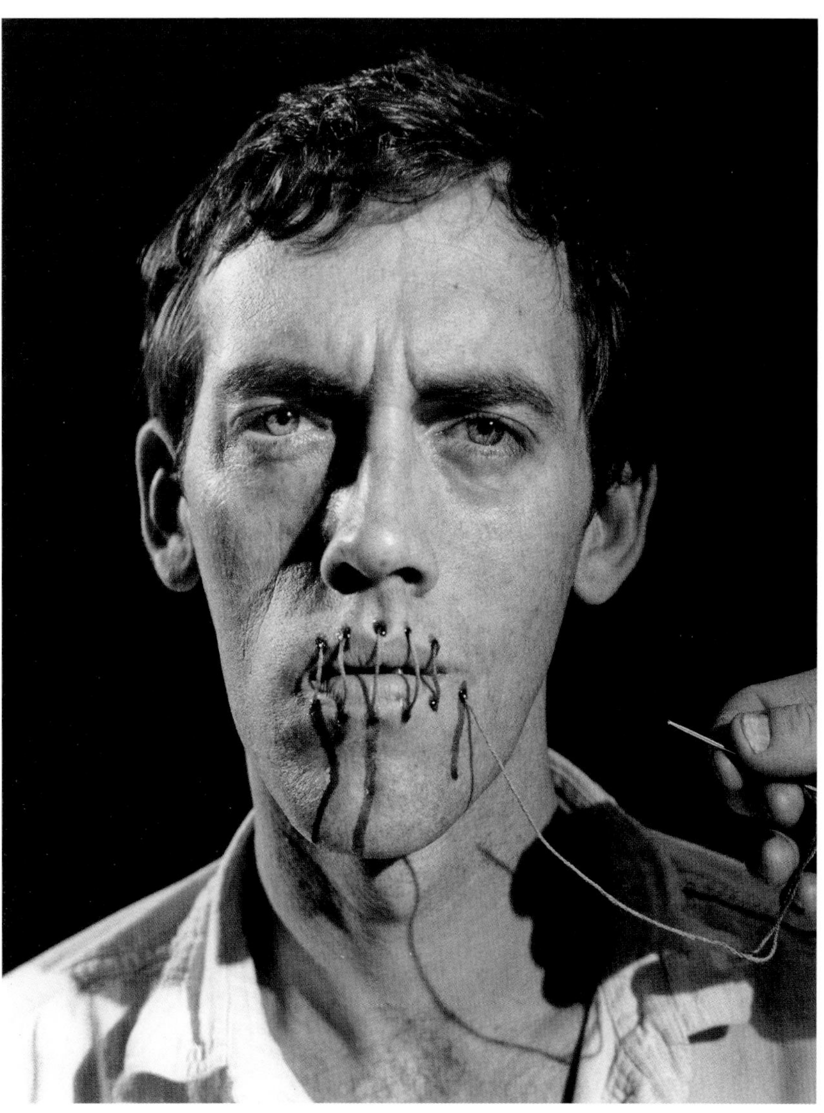

Andreas Sterzing, *David Wojnarowicz (Silence = Death)*, 1989

PHILIP-LORCA diCORCIA

Eddie Anderson; 21 Years Old; Houston, Texas; $20, 1990–92

A tableau of estrangement in dreamy California

Point of view: you're sitting in a diner on Santa Monica Boulevard in Los Angeles at dusk with the essentials of all-American nourishment – hamburger, cup of joe – before you. Maybe you've just selected a song from the jukebox. Looking through the window, you see a young man, his sun-kissed body outlined against a dusky Angelino sky. In that moment, the window of the diner changes into a shop window: the young man is advertising himself as a consumer good, another item on the menu. This image, from Philip-Lorca diCorcia's iconic *Hustlers* series (1990–92), is no happenstance; it's one of a series of staged real-world dioramas featuring male drifters and drug addicts. DiCorcia would carefully select a location, preparing the shot with Polaroids, then approach a subject and offer to take his picture. As recorded in the title, he would negotiate a fee equal to what the man would have charged for sex – a provocative response to the atmosphere of bigoted anti-homosexual panic that had spread at the height of the AIDS epidemic. This is no attempt at documentary truth; it's the invention of a constructed, artificial authenticity. Judgment is withheld, interpretation left open, mystery total.

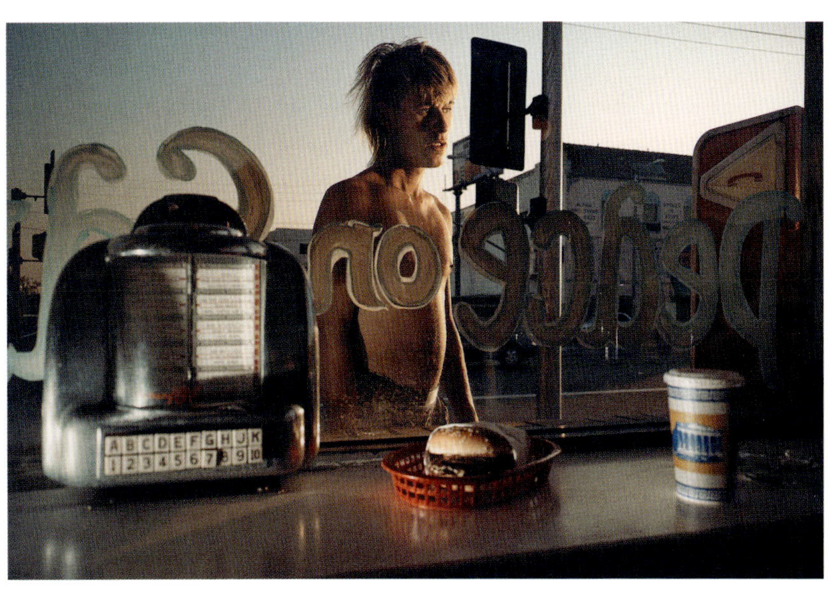

Philip-Lorca diCorcia, *Eddie Anderson; 21 Years Old; Houston, Texas; $20*, 1990–92, chromogenic print, 60×91 cm

GILLIAN WEARING

I'M DESPERATE, 1992-3

Street photography becomes public therapy

A photographer stood in a busy street in south London and approached passers-by, asking them to write down what's on their minds and hold their statement up to her camera. Many agreed. 'I think the idea was very appealing,' the photographer in question, Gillian Wearing, said. The young man in the suit complied with her request, expressing a sentiment at odds with his outward appearance as a picture of corporate ambition, and which seemed, Wearing later said, to surprise even himself. With the series S*igns that say what you want them to say and not Signs that say what someone else wants you to say* (1992–93), Wearing found a new approach to street photography, where her subjects participated in the composition of their image and gave it some meaning of their own, like a caption. This allowed for a confessional moment of clarity, an expressive and transgressive dialogue between public image and private identity, something Wearing has gone on to explore further in her later work using masks and disguises.

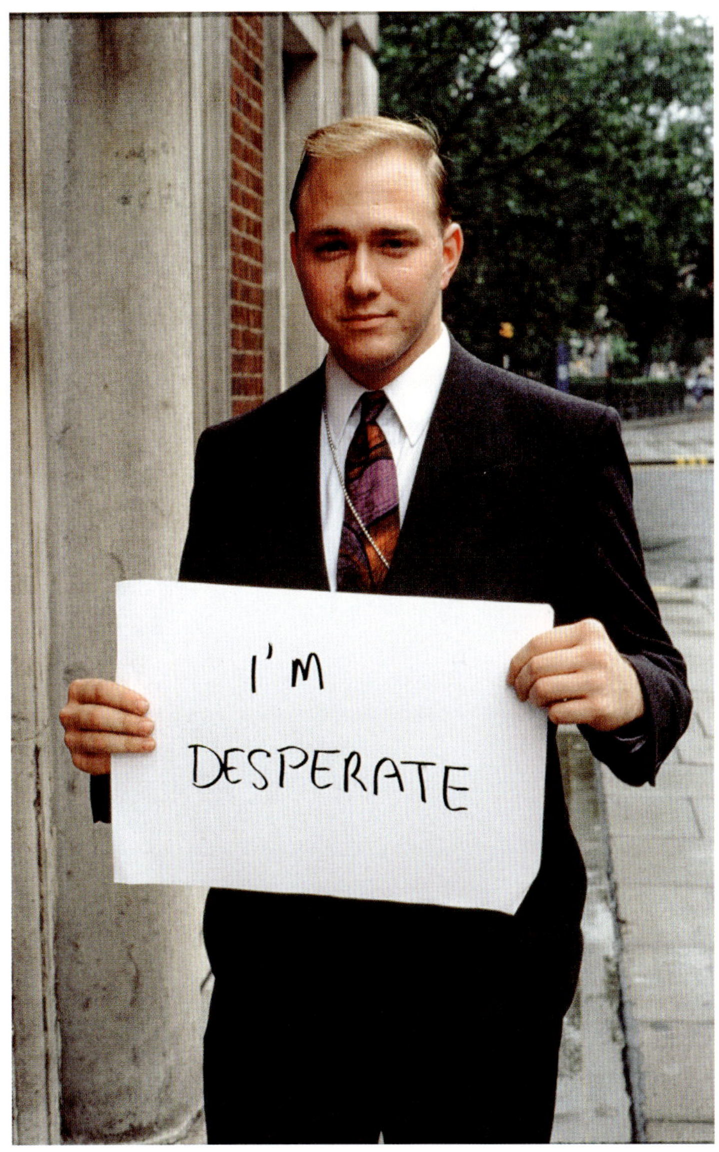

Gillian Wearing, *Signs that say what you want them to say and not Signs that say what someone else wants you to say I'M DESPERATE*, 1992-3

HIROSHI SUGIMOTO

Union City Drive-In, Union City, 1993

Time capsule UFO is a matter of life and death

Japanese photographer Hiroshi Sugimoto is a sort of illusionist. He has, for example, produced dramatically lit black-and-white photographs of natural history dioramas where there is a troubling suggestion that the stuffed animals are in fact alive: 'However fake the subject, once photographed, it's as good as real,' Sugimoto has observed. This image is part of his series of photographs of cinema screens, *Theaters*, begun in the late 1970s. The idea for the project came to him in a 'near-hallucinatory vision' when he asked himself what a whole movie shot in a single frame would look like and came up with the answer: 'You get a shining screen.' He calculated that a two-hour film is made up of 172,800 still images, and turned them all into one. By opening the camera shutter for the length of the entire film screening, Sugimoto allowed the images to fuse, creating an unidentified alien object, a white glowing entity from another world, a portal to another dimension. Time has been magically compressed, but in this open-air cinema, there is a clue in the sky, where light trails across the dark reveal some hours have passed. This isn't about finding Cartier-Bresson's 'decisive moment'; it's about creating an image that exists in its own realm and shows something that no one but the camera has seen.

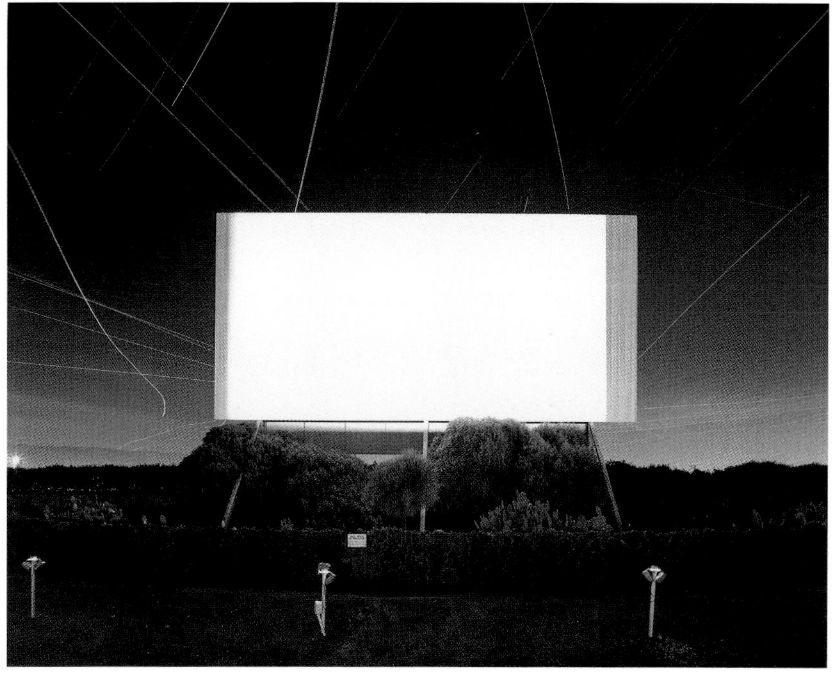

Hiroshi Sugimoto, *Union City Drive-In, Union City*, 1993, gelatin silver print, 47 × 60.4 cm

WOLFGANG TILLMANS

last still-life, NY, 1995

Beautiful detritus suggests it's later than you think

There is something of the archivist about German photographer Wolfgang Tillmans. His eye notices everything, and no element of his past is trivial. A chronicler of the lives of the exuberant gay and club scenes of the 1990s, he also produced a series of meditative windowsill still lifes tracking the places he visited all over the world. Though it clearly refers to a highly prized fine-art tradition – the still-life fruit paintings of 17th-century Spanish and Dutch artists – Tillmans' image transforms the genre, making it grittier, less precious and more democratic. Tillmans is anti-materialistic in his political stance and finds casual beauty in everyday clutter. This shot contrasts colourful, vitamin-laden fruit and evidence of less healthful pursuits: the poison and the antidote. The image also has the air of a vanitas still life, where a 17th-century artist would have had a skull in his composition as a reminder of mortality; with Tillmans, it's ash and extinguished cigarette butts.

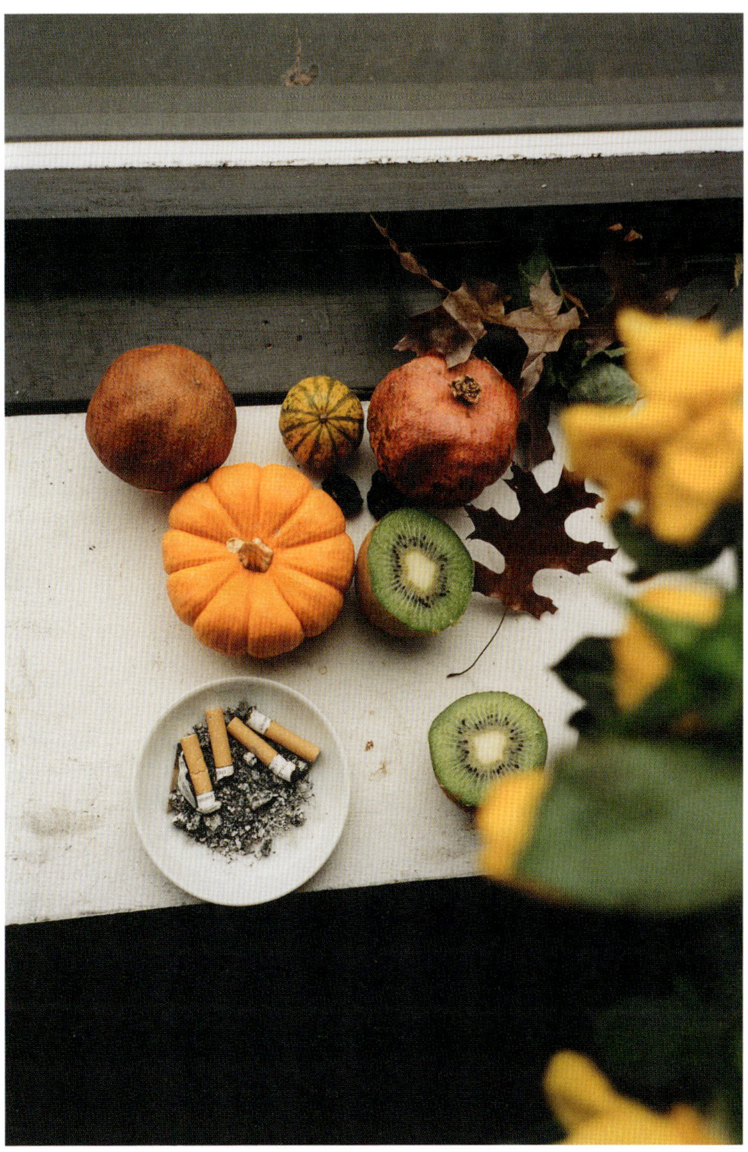

Wolfgang Tillmans, *last still-life*, NY, 1995

MARTIN PARR

Benidorm, Spain, 1997

Sun worshipper is put under the microscope

When he first visited the Spanish resort of Benidorm in 1997, British photographer Martin Parr was smitten: 'I loved it. I think the impact it made on me when I first went was partially because I'd never seen such a busy, crazy resort.' Parr is a fascinated observer of human behaviour on the beach, where people relax and lose their inhibitions. To make the most of Benidorm and its crowd of sun worshippers in all their saturated multicoloured glory, Parr used a daytime ring flash and a macro lens, equipment more normally used by the medical profession, which allowed him to go in forensically close. There is something anthropological, as well as a little kitsch and satirical, about this portrait of a lady reclining against the intense blue background of her towel, her eyes covered with tiny blue plastic shields, pierced with slits for looking out through. The sunbather's expression is serious, determined; she's entirely focused on enjoying her holiday. 'It's easier and more rewarding to shoot older people,' Parr said. 'They have more character.'

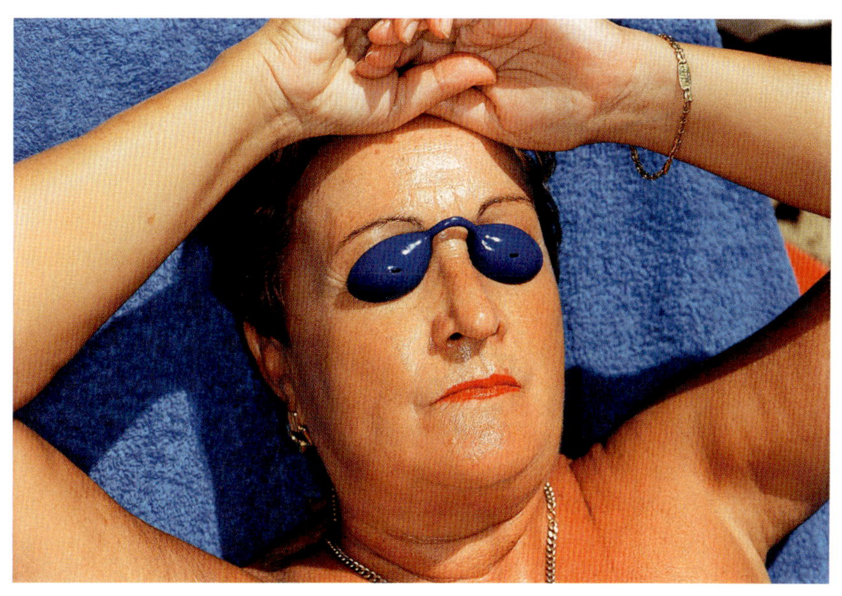

Martin Parr, *Benidorm, Spain*, 1997

EDWARD BURTYNSKY

Oxford Tire Pile #1, Westley, California, 1999

Blighted landscape achieves new toxic radiance

'I'm looking at humans and what they're doing to the planet as if I were an alien,' Edward Burtynsky said of his work documenting industrially altered landscapes. Mirroring the enormity of his subject matter, his photography is about monumental scale, as in this transfixing image of mountains of discarded tyres in California. It is part of Burtynsky's *Oil* series, inspired by a sudden realisation that everything he had ever photographed, right down to the film he used, had been made possible by oil – a source of progress and energy as well as a source of destruction of our natural habitat. Here, Burtynsky performs a visual trick, seducing the eye with a sumptuous, awe-inspiring image of accumulation while at the same time forcing us to see something we prefer not to think about. Yes, there is something of a cornucopia about the image, but its point is that in car-centred America, piles of tyres have monstrously substituted themselves for natural hills. Shortly after this shot was taken, the tyre dump was struck by lightning and a fire burned for a month, releasing contaminants into the atmosphere. An environmental clean-up of the site was completed in 2007 at a cost of $20 million.

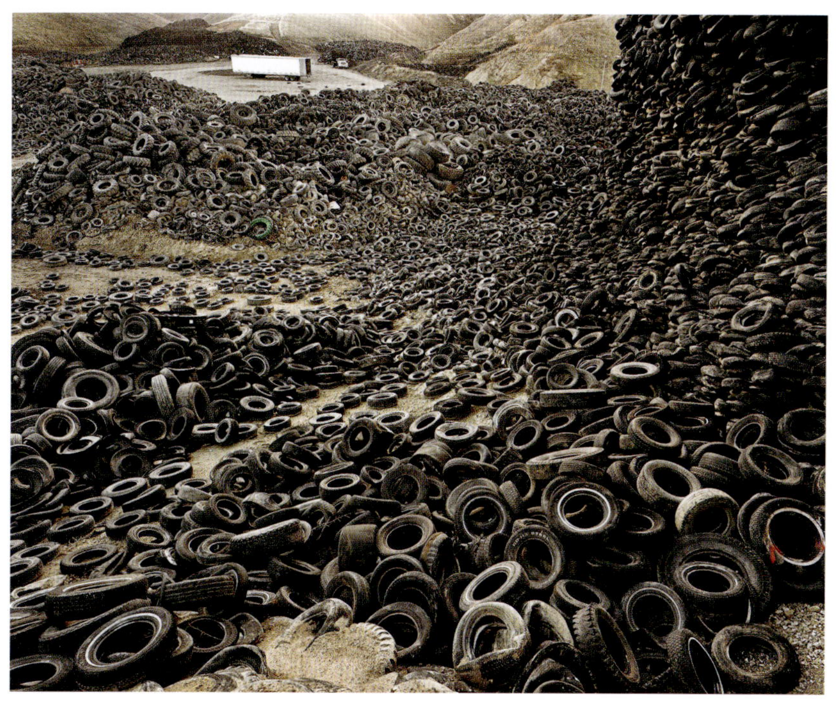

Edward Burtynsky, *Oxford Tire Pile #1, Westley, California*, 1999

TODD HIDO

House Hunting #2424-B, 1999

Anybody home? Home is where alienation lives

While driving at night around anonymous suburban streets on the West Coast of America, Todd Hido (originally from Ohio) became fascinated by the enigmatic, melancholy, closed-off presence of the houses he saw. The series *House Hunting*, whose subversive title hints at the photographer's predatory gaze, looks at a decaying, worn-out suburban America, cold and unwelcoming. Though Hido never concealed himself when photographing the houses that interested him – often those that, like this one, showed a light in the windows behind closed blinds – some owners felt that he was trespassing and sometimes called the police. 'If you want to take a photo,' Hido says, 'you don't knock on someone's door to ask permission.' Hido captures California looking eerily unlike itself: it has snowed; an ethereal fog is rising from the ocean. You tune into this, wondering about the people living in the house. Then you wonder: is the house real? It is so minimalist, with no trace of picturesque ornamentation, that even with the lights on it looks as empty as a model or a stage set.

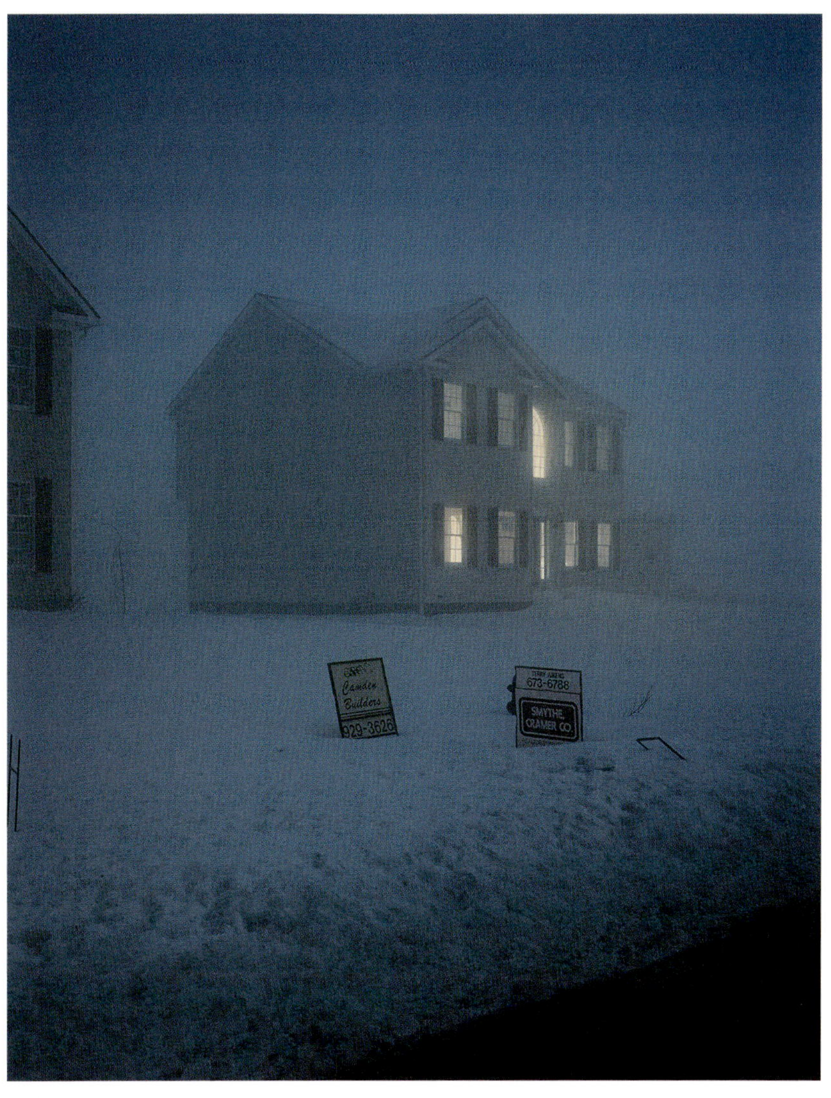

Todd Hido, *House Hunting, #2424-B*, 1999

JEFF WALL

After 'Invisible Man' by Ralph Ellison, the Prologue, 1999–2000

A luminous tableau of exclusion

It isn't often that a modern artist chooses to illustrate a piece of writing, let alone achieves this level of transmutation. This layered piece, taking Jeff Wall a long time to assemble in his Vancouver studio, is a response to Ralph Ellison's 1952 novel *Invisible Man*, about a young Black man recounting his experience of racism. Annulled by other people's gazes to the point of feeling invisible, he retreats to a forgotten underground room in a whites-only building on the edge of Harlem. Wall translates a spare piece of fiction into a maximalist visual statement teeming with domestic clutter. Ellison's novel has little description save for one detail: the 1,369 bulbs fitted on the ceiling of the underground room and operated by power stolen from the city's electric grid. Is it any wonder that the invisible man desires light? In Wall's photograph the profusion of light bulbs, like a deconstructed, collapsing chandelier, bring to the scene an air of magic realism. Displayed in a light box like an advertising billboard to catch our attention, the photograph's cinematic scale endows Wall's outcast with the grandeur traditionally reserved for subjects of Old Masters paintings.

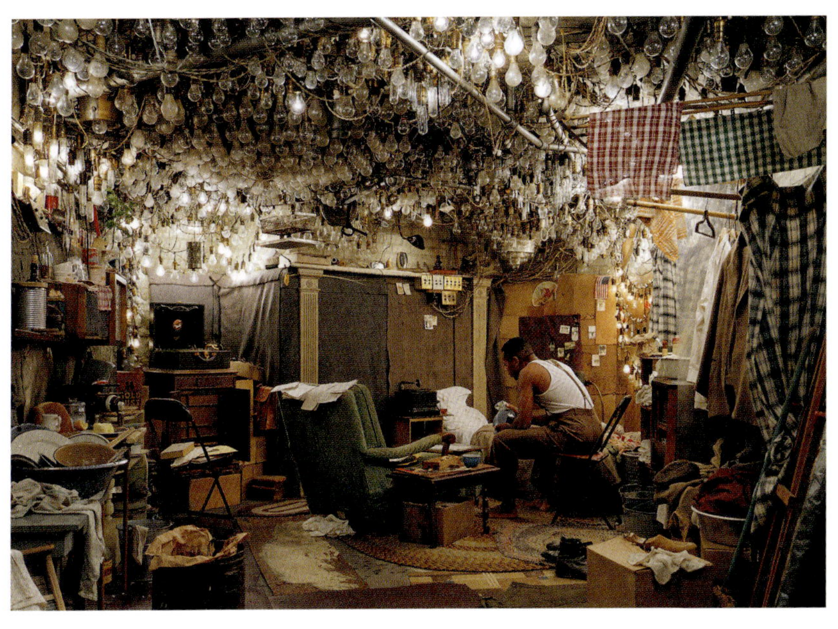

Jeff Wall, *After 'Invisible Man' by Ralph Ellison, the Prologue*, 1999–2000, silver dye bleach transparency; aluminium light box, The Museum of Modern Art, New York

ROGER BALLEN

Show Off, 2000

A moment's anarchic joy in the wilderness of the margins

'A good picture comes from nowhere,' according to Roger Ballen. Here, he captures a moment of vivid physical expressiveness: a jubilant-looking man strikes an explosive pose, obscuring another man who appears to be on the phone and is seemingly unaffected by his gesture. The image is immediately disorientating, destabilising. Where are we? People and furniture are featured, but how are we meant to read and interpret their presence? Behind the two men, a wire hangs from a couple of nails and there are tentative drawings on the wall. What is this place? Ballen is dedicated to 'exploring the shadow side of life' and has focused much of his photography on a recurring cast of social outcasts he met and befriended in rural South Africa, and on their dilapidated surroundings. This is a poverty-stricken, skeletal world that is strongly evocative of Samuel Beckett's theatre of the absurd, with its aimless, suffering characters trapped in a surreal dead-end life. When you look at the image again, the presence of the wires adds something mechanical to the man's movements. The image suggests an unexplained, hallucinatory moment of joy: showing off on an empty stage.

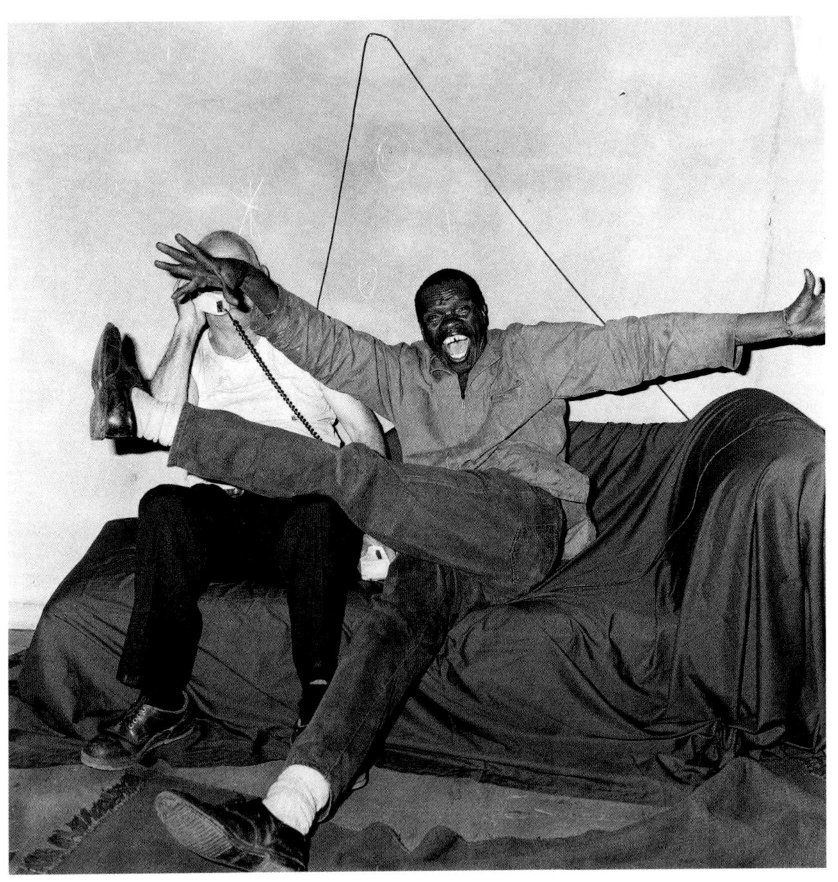

Roger Ballen, *Show Off*, 2000

ANDREAS GURSKY

Shanghai, 2000

Hovering inside the Tower of Babel

It isn't immediately obvious where we are: is it the interior of a machine or some sort of gigantic theatre? A prison, maybe? No, this is in fact the atrium of the Grand Hyatt hotel in Shanghai, situated at the top of the 88-floor Jin Mao Tower. German photographer Andreas Gursky produces large, immersive and impassively critical images that speak of global capitalism. Alongside warehouses, apartment buildings and office blocks, the lobbies of luxury hotels interest him as examples of the architecture of wealth and power. Here, a towering interior has been made even more vertical and vertiginous through digital editing. Gursky shot the same image from three different floors and made them into a single image, evening out the colour tone for maximum golden-yellow radiance. The effect is like hovering inside the Tower of Babel. Though we see a glimpse of the floor, the cropping of the image suggests that the structure might continue to rise forever. It is futuristic and inspiring, but at the same time the artificial light and architectural repetitiveness induce claustrophobia. Therein lies the paradox of globalist achievements.

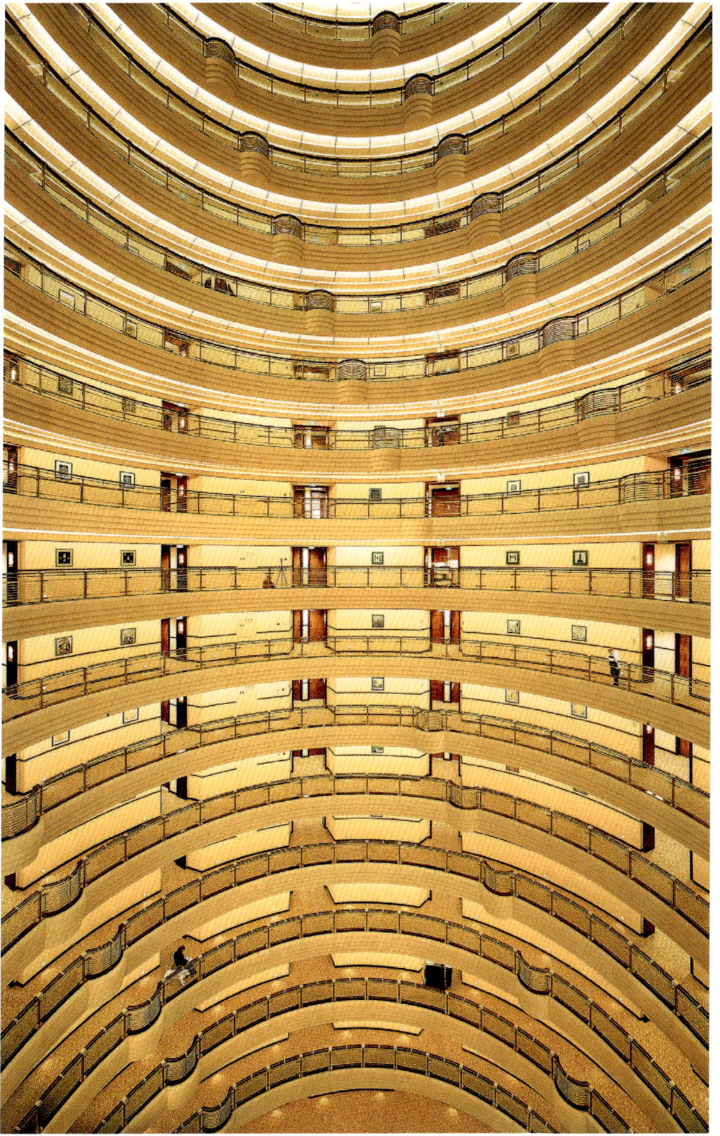

Andreas Gursky, *Shanghai*, 2000

ALEX WEBB

Outside of the Blue Mosque during Ramadan, 2001

Street photography meets fine art in a moment of suspense

It was when American photographer Alex Webb began to travel far afield, to Mexico, the Caribbean Islands, Africa and Asia, that he embraced colour as his medium: 'Searing light and intense colour seemed somewhat embedded in the cultures that I had begun working in, so utterly different than the gray-brown reticence of my New England background.' But to Webb, colour is also a way of capturing and expressing emotions and states of consciousness through resonant, open-ended images such as this one. Here, the iconic Blue Mosque in Istanbul, Turkey, is cropped beyond recognition in order to frame a small incident tinged with anxiety: at dusk, a small boy stands at the gate, watchful, perhaps waiting for someone; behind him are the blurred silhouettes of a man and a woman who may or may not be his parents. As the evening light bathes the marble walls and what we glimpse of an inner courtyard, the child stands amid blocks of vivid green and terracotta red traversed by strong shadows and overhanging chains. Beneath those, the boy's pastel-pink candyfloss looks incongruously cloudlike, almost a supernatural phenomenon. The image is a question, not an answer.

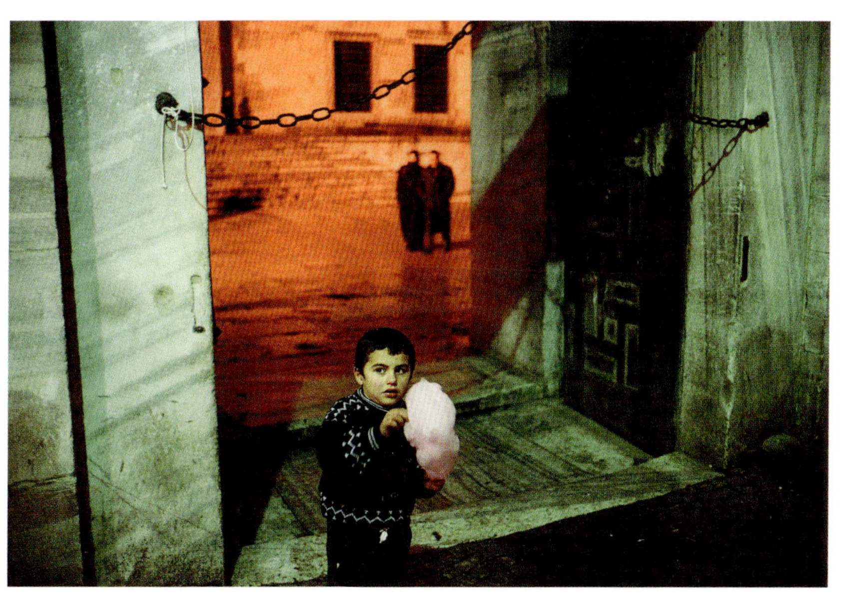

Alex Webb, *Outside of the Blue Mosque during Ramadan*, 2001

ALEC SOTH

Charles, Vasa, Minnesota, 2002

Portrait of an American dreamer

From 1999 to 2002, Minnesota native Alec Soth took several road trips along the Mississippi River and photographed the strangers he met en route. The result was his 2004 book, *Sleeping by the Mississippi*, an exploration of a zone between reality and dream, of which this portrait is the signature image. Having spotted from the road a house with a strange glass room on top of it, Soth knocked on the door and met Charles, the eccentric owner who had built the room as his 'cockpit', and his wife, who explained that he had also moved the staircase in their house three times, because that was the sort of person he was. A flight enthusiast in a flying suit (apparently his habitual outfit), Charles holds in his hands two model aeroplanes painted in the colours of the American flag, which he made with his daughters. Soth's image feels at once like a face-on documentary portrait of a Midwesterner living on the margins and like a memory from a poetic dream.

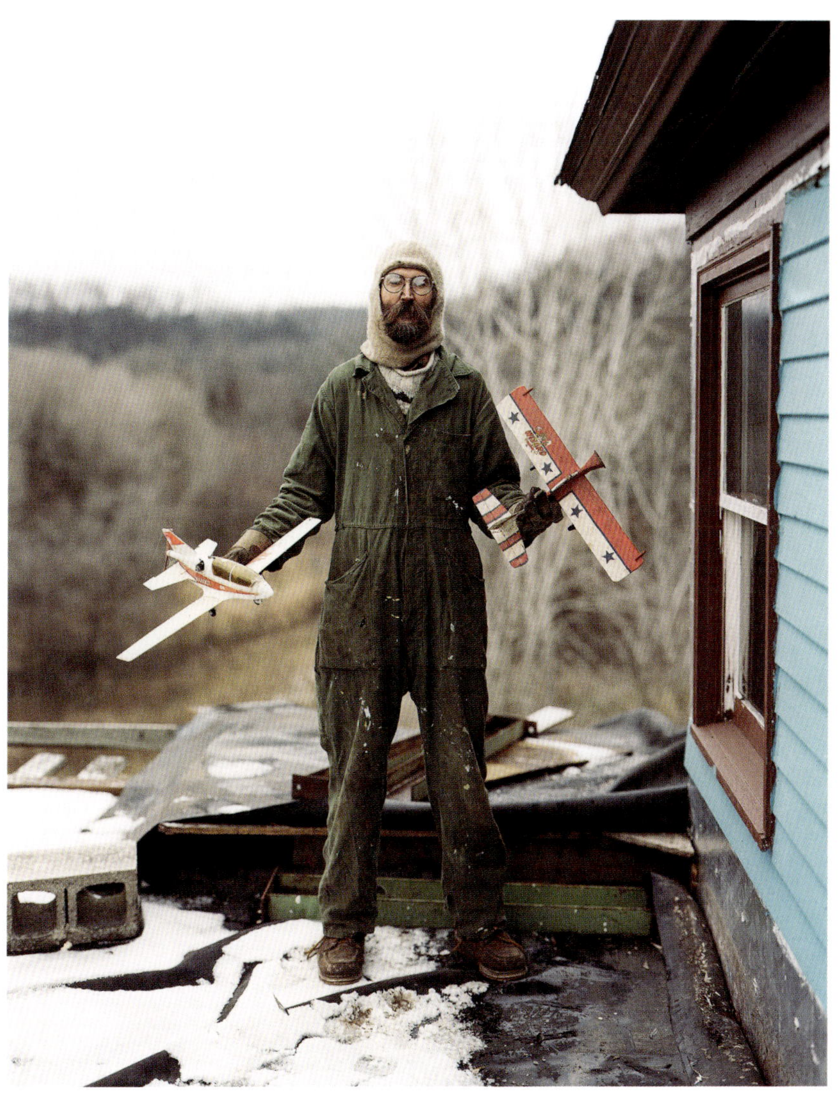

Alec Soth, *Charles, Vasa, Minnesota*, 2002

ELLEN VON UNWERTH

Peaches, Rouilly le Bas, 2002

Erotica as triumphant dreamworld

Just three girlfriends hanging out in the countryside having a snack. But wait: the image is saturated with sauciness – stockings! Juicy peaches! – almost to the point of pastiche. Though the women are glamorous and their hitched-up skirts provocative, they are also relaxed and comfortable, either absorbed in their own thoughts or (in the case of the woman on the far right) sending a cool mocking gaze our way. Ellen von Unwerth grew up in foster homes, dreaming of fairy tales and the circus – where she worked for a time before becoming a fashion model and then a photographer. In her photographs, she constructs a fantasy world of her own infused with the triumphant sexuality of larger-than-life film stars like Brigitte Bardot, 1940s pin-ups and the kitsch exuberance of burlesque. It defined the commercial and editorial visual style of the 1990s and 2000s. Having personally experienced how restrictive a model's experience can be, von Unwerth consciously injects a sense of freedom and spontaneity into her own photography, casting over her models the female gaze of a playful instigator. The result is images such as this one, glorying in knowing, actively acknowledged eroticism.

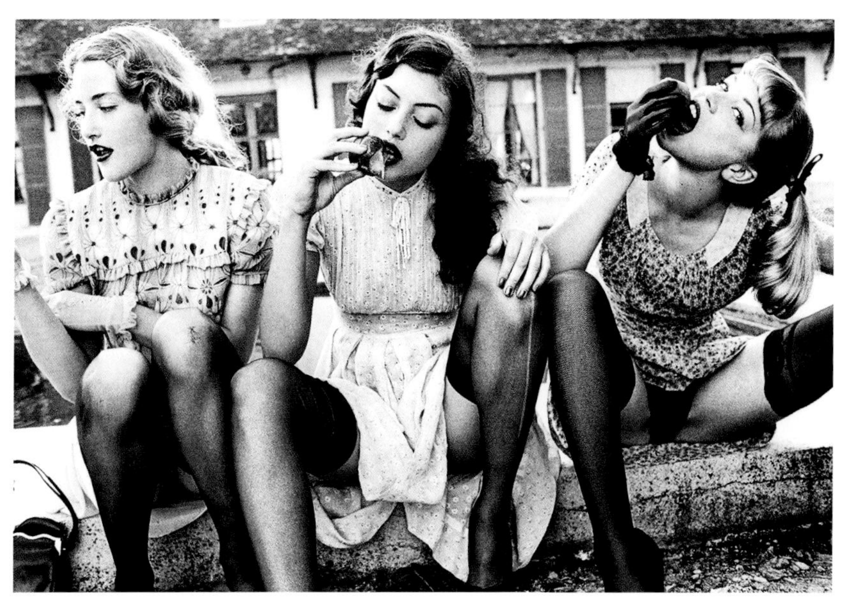

Ellen von Unwerth, *Peaches, Rouilly le Bas*, 2002

SEBASTIÃO SALGADO

Marine Iguana, Galápagos Islands, Ecuador, 2004

Non-human image dreams of a time before the Fall

'I want to see if I can put a kind of virginity in these pictures, if you can say that,' Brazilian social documentarist and photo-journalist Sebastião Salgado said of his *Genesis* series, an eight-year photographic project about what remains of Earth's beauty in unspoiled places from Siberia to the Brazilian rainforest. Photographed during Salgado's extended stay in the National Park of the Galápagos, the clawed animal foot confidently gripping the rock belongs to a protected species, the marine iguana. 'They are giant lizards, or tiny dinosaurs, with claws like diamanté gloves,' Salgado said. Indeed, it is possible to imagine such reptilian gloves as the work of Surrealist fashion designer Elsa Schiaparelli or, in their dramatic black-and-white, something from interplanetary science fiction. But Salgado's work is driven by his love of planet Earth. This image expresses his fascination with a singular earthly creature and its evolution from living on land to learning to swim and dive, feeding on algae and drinking salt water. The photograph is expressive of Salgado's enthusiastic environmentalist philosophy: alongside his photographic career, he runs Instituto Terra, where he is rebuilding and rewilding a rainforest in Brazil.

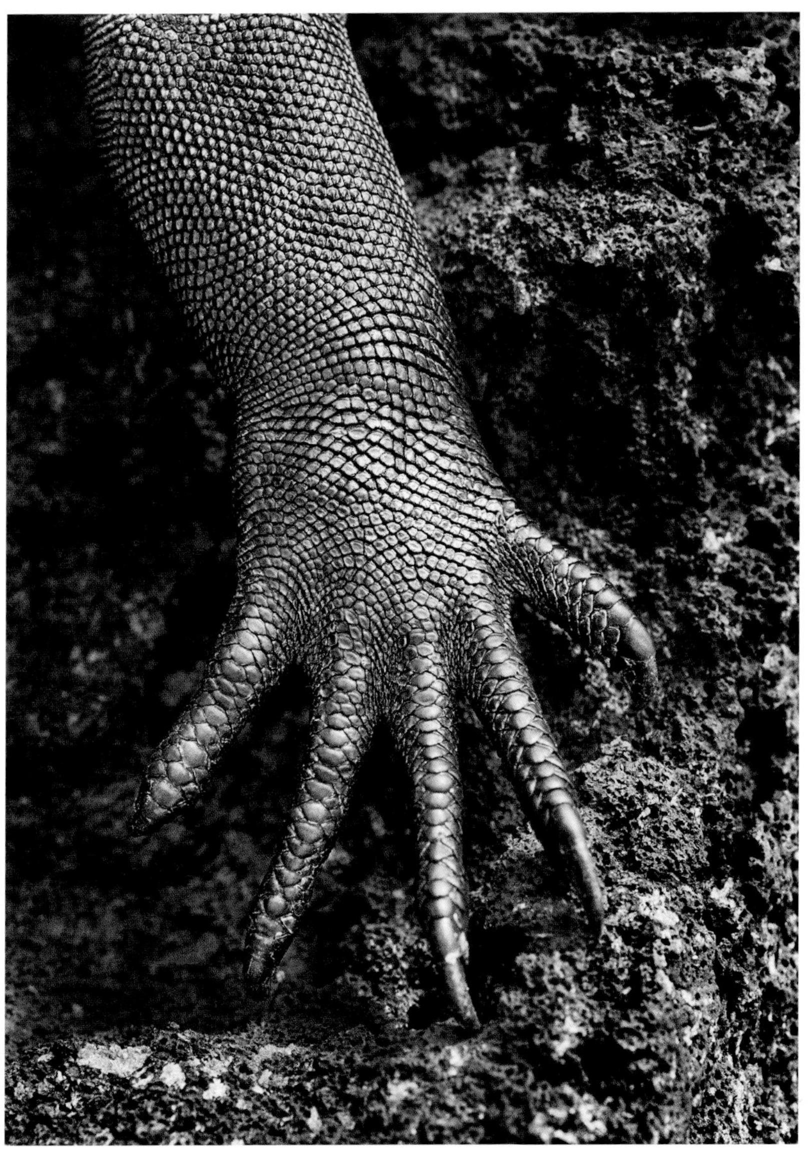

Sebastião Salgado, *Marine Iguana, Galápagos Islands, Ecuador*, 2004, gelatin silver print, 50.8 × 40.64 cm

TIM WALKER

Lily Cole and Spiral Staircase, 2005

Fashion visionary manufactures enchanted otherworld

'Fashion photography,' said Tim Walker, 'is the dream department of photography.' Walker occupies a position in an English surreal-Romantic photographic tradition. This otherworldly image – shot for British *Vogue* – of Lily Cole halfway up a spiral staircase in a vaporous ice-blue Stella McCartney gown is emblematic of his style and method. Walker was on holiday in India when he found the location, a crumbling palace that had been hit by an earthquake years before. Robin Derrick, then art director at *Vogue*, described Walker showing the fashion director a snapshot of the rusting staircase 'with a marker pen sketch over it of a girl standing in a long dress'. For Walker's vision to be realised completely in the shoot, the dress had to be made in just the right shade to match the powdery blue of the peeling hallway, and the right length and weight to hang down from the staircase and drape as elegantly as Walker intended, acquiring an almost architectural identity. Far less important than the product featured – the designer garment itself – is the imagined narrative underpinning the image. This is fashion photography as a means of creating a parallel universe, a lavish, perfect world.

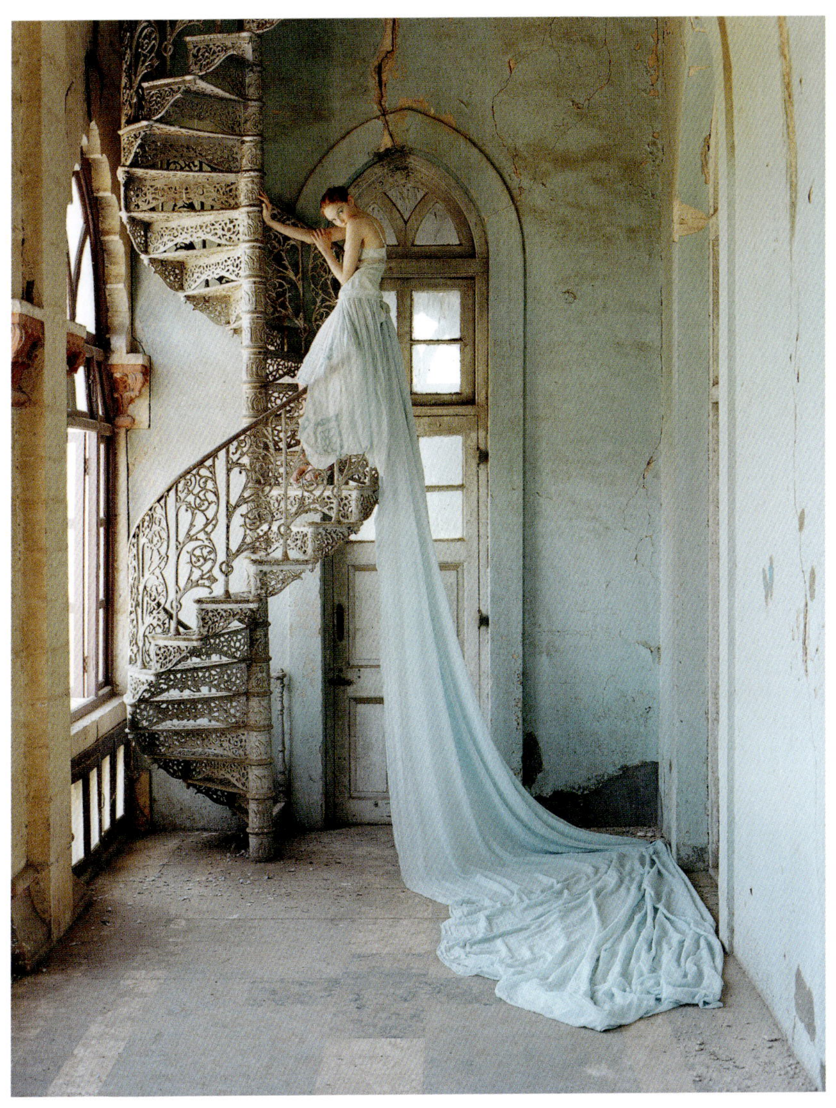

Tim Walker, *Lily Cole and Spiral Staircase*, 2005

MATT GOINS

Flying Jockey, 2006

Photographer stops time; man on horse defies gravity

This is one of the greatest examples of adrenaline-fuelled sports photography. On the day when he caught this shot on the fly, Matt Goins was not even supposed to be at the track because he was recovering from an appendectomy. But by an incredible stroke of luck, he was covering the race at Keeneland, Kentucky, and standing just 20 feet away when apprentice jockey Julien Leparoux vaulted over the head of his horse, Sanibel Storm. Ejected from the saddle, Leparoux is flying. He immediately afterwards somersaulted into the infield racing track, but he and Sanibal Storm were unhurt. In this breathless image, with other horses going full pelt in the background, Leparoux is coming right at us, so foreshortened in that airborne split second that he bears a passing resemblance to a yellow and green ladybird. Goins had been a commercial photographer for 15 years when this thrilling image won him the Eclipse Award for coverage of thoroughbred racing.

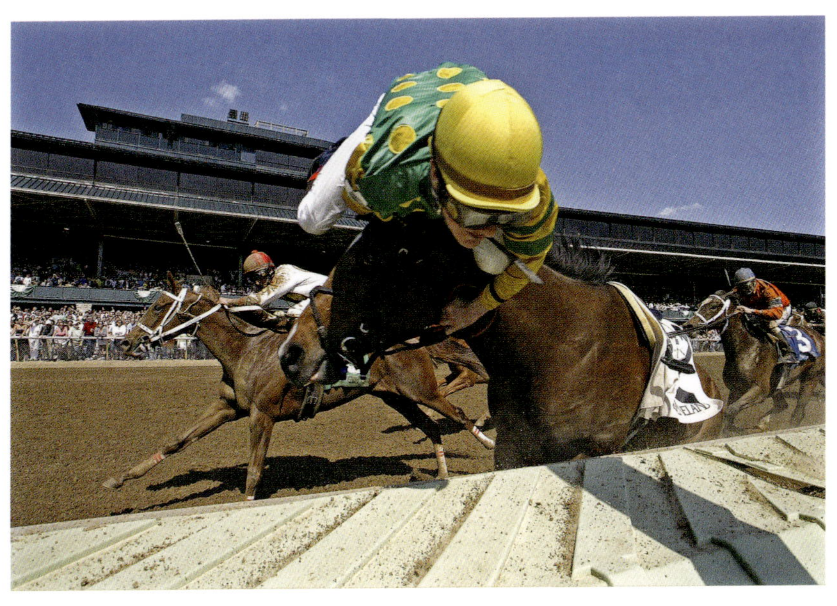

Matt Goins, *Flying Jockey*, 2006

NADAV KANDER

Yibin I (Bathers) Sichuan Province, 2007

Dystopian landscape photography flirts with the sublime

This image of a group of male swimmers in the Sichuan province of China captures a face-off between nature and industrialisation. The composition is eloquent: the diagonal lines of the monumental rockface, elemental and prehistoric, prolonged by the smaller rock where the men stand, jut into the frame on a downward slope. Across the water, an industrial plant spews chemical fumes into the atmosphere. One of the men holds a buoy, but will it be enough to keep them safe in this faintly post-apocalyptic world? Nadav Kander set out to photograph the length of the vast Yangtze and the people who live along its banks (one in every 18 people on the planet) because he believes the river is much more than a waterway, 'embedded in the consciousness of the Chinese' and running 'in the blood of the people'. It also affords front-row seats to the astonishing spectacle of China's constructive and destructive industrial and economic change. The small size of the human figures, dwarfed by nature as in a 19th-century painting by Caspar David Friedrich, also suggests the insignificance of individuals in the face of the state and its policies.

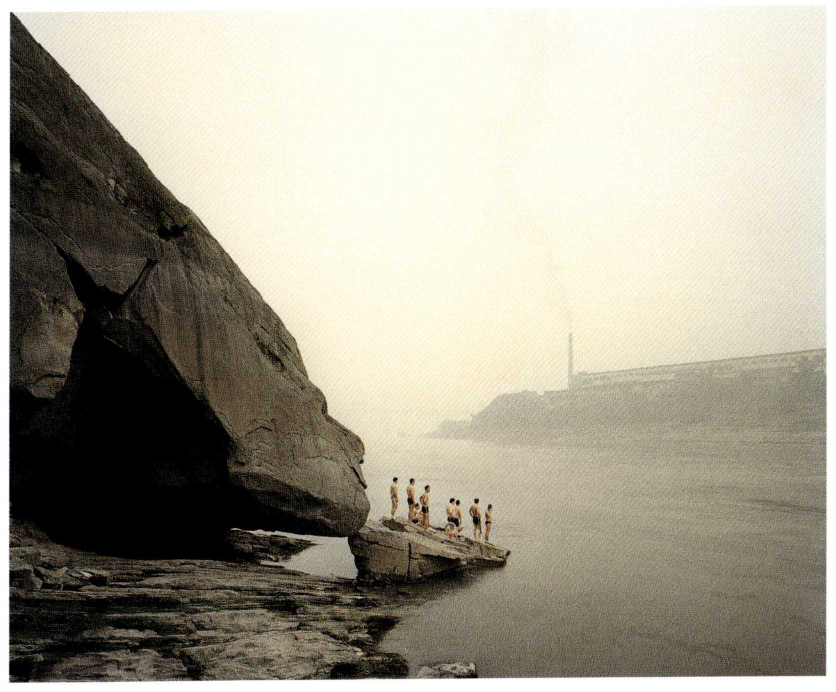

Nadav Kander, *Yibin I (Bathers) Sichuan Province*, 2007, chromogenic colour print, 96 × 122.5 cm

MICHAEL WOLF

Tokyo Compression #05, 2009

How many commuters can you fit into a train?

'They couldn't do anything because they were immobilised like sardines,' German photographer Michael Wolf said about his series *Tokyo Compression*, the expressive and uncomfortable portraits that he photographed at Shimokitazawa station over a four-year period. The subjects are trapped inside overcrowded trains at rush hour, their faces pressed against the windows, at which point it's too late to refuse to be photographed. A photojournalist turned artist with a strong sense of his work as being akin to that of an anthropologist, Wolf is documenting – and intruding into – a hellish everyday experience which, in the context of a hyperdense megacity where the only affordable housing is miles out of the centre, must be endured. There is something powerfully dehumanising about the crush, which this photograph intensifies by obscuring the commuter's eyes. We don't know what he's thinking about, if he's praying or shutting his eyes pretending that the photographer isn't there. The whole world has shrunk down to this: the clammy condensation on the window, the salaryman's tie, his closed-mouth rictus and the pores of his skin, pressed against the glass like a specimen in a Petri dish.

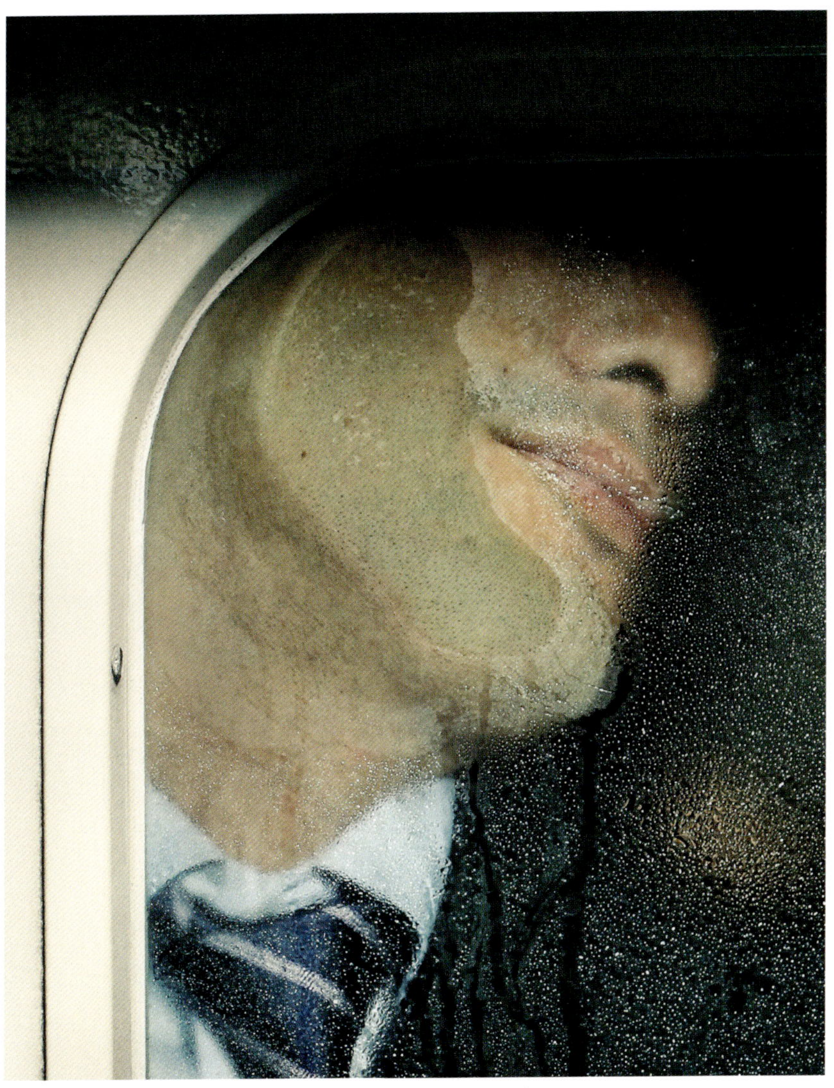

Michael Wolf, *Tokyo Compression #05*, 2009, chromogenic colour print, 51 × 41 cm

HARRY GRUYAERT

A Traveller in Charles de Gaulle Airport, 2010

Solo sunlit alienation in liminal space

Airports hold a fascination for Belgian photographer Harry Gruyaert. They present him with 'the interplay of light, transparency and reflections, the overlapping layers that make you lose your bearings and create a very strong impression of being caught between two worlds', and they operate as stage sets 'with hosts of players gliding through' on the move or, as in this image, waiting for their flight. Airports exist physically; they are made of concrete and glass. But they are only places of transit, antechambers, waiting rooms – not real places. The man sitting in this airport lounge is only passing through; by definition, as a traveller, his presence will be transitory, ghostlike. The vast hangar in which he sits is also given definition by the graphic lines and colours of modern design. Airports can be places of stress and anxiety, of rushing and being unpleasantly processed. But not here. It is perhaps because the man is alone, enjoying a moment of privacy, that in spite of the cage-like patterning of shadows on the floor, the image provides a sense of peace and serenity, of colourful dreaminess.

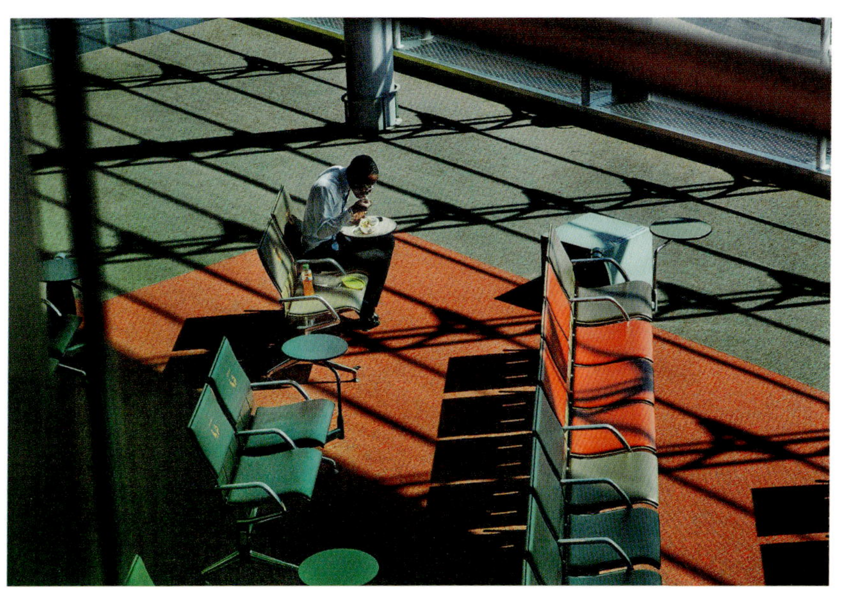

Harry Gruyaert, *A Traveller in Charles de Gaulle Airport*, 2010

VIVIANE SASSEN

Parasomnia, 2010

Dreamweaver stages anti-portrait in impossible space

Darkness is traditionally associated with sleep and light with lucid consciousness – but not in Dutch photographer Viviane Sassen's series *Parasomnia*, shot in East and West Africa. In this image, a scorching light intensifying all colours – red T-shirt, blue chair, yellow stripes on shorts – shines on a young boy seemingly asleep on the ground while, absurdly, sitting on a plastic chair. Did he fall over? Or float up a wall? Has the world turned on its axis? 'Parasomnia' refers to abnormal sleeping behaviour such as night terrors and sleepwalking. It is that liminal space between sleep and wakefulness that Sassen explores in her carefully staged scenes. Having spent her childhood years in Kenya, she has said she felt like a foreigner when she returned to the Netherlands; at the same time, she was always aware of being an outsider in Africa. Perhaps this sense of dislocation is what feeds her photographs, like visions conjured from a dream state. As is often the case in her images, the subject's face is averted, a hint that Sassen is consciously resisting the conventions of European portraits of Africans, whether they dwell on misery or happiness.

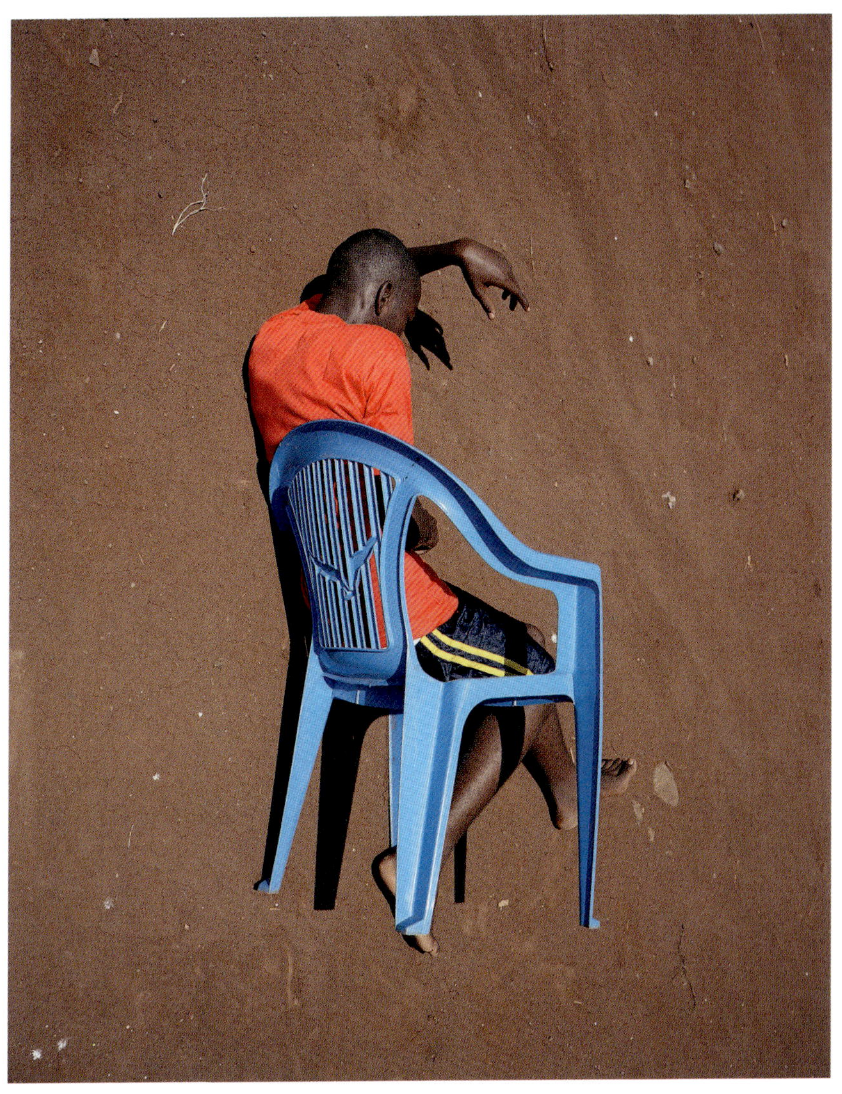

Viviane Sassen, *Parasomnia*, 2010

RINKO KAWAUCHI

Untitled, *from the series* Illuminance, 2011

Woman's gaze turns flower into a star

Can a flower be dazzled by light? Yes, it can – in Rinko Kawauchi's sensitised world. In the act of taking a photograph, focusing on a small element of nature, Kawauchi feels that she reconnects with feelings of wonder experienced in childhood. She shows us a world caught in the radiance of paradise, where a flower could conceivably appear sentient. Drawing in part on her interest in Shinto and Buddhism, she calls her images of nature 'prayers invisible to the eye' and sees them as instruments for meditation on the meaning of life, as open windows allowing us to consider where we are in our own journey. But the experience is not always one of serene contemplation: unease sometimes lurks in the image, a frisson of fear. If Kawauchi's photo 'speaks' to us, is it saying that the flower is radiant, or that it is painfully dazzled, almost annulled by the excess of light? 'There is still more unknown than known,' she notes. Life is fleeting, and the natural world a subtle, disturbing mystery.

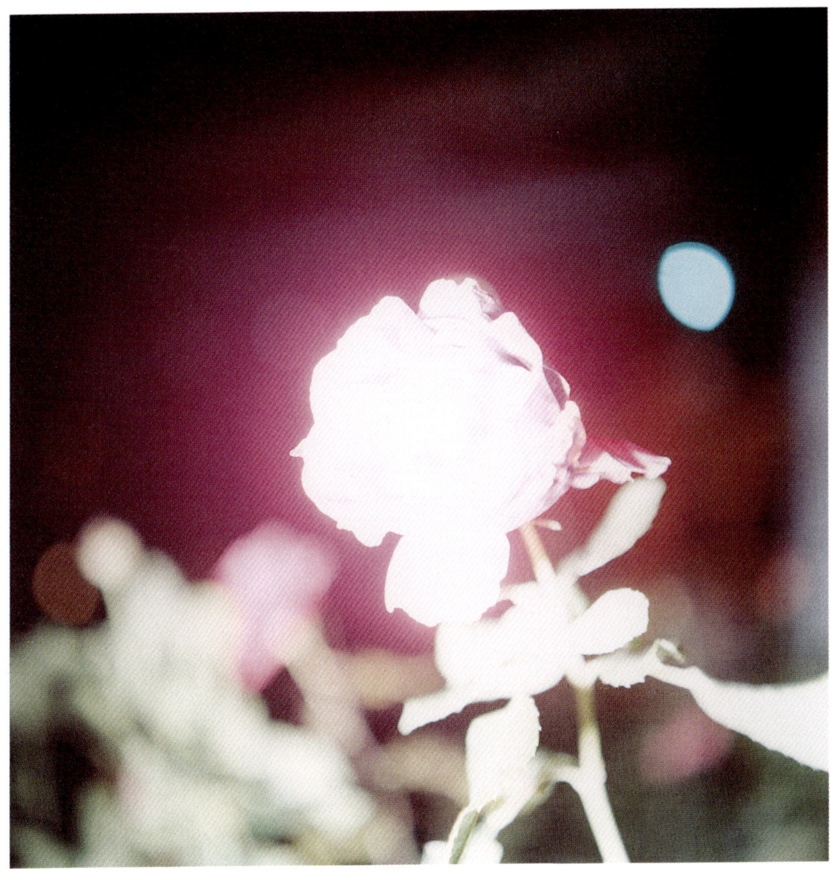

Rinko Kawauchi, *Untitled*, from the series *Illuminance*, 2011

ALEX PRAGER

Crowd #2 (Emma), 2012

The crowd that is not quite real, not quite fake

'It's not like recreations of real crowds,' American artist Alex Prager has said about her series of large-scale crowd scenes. 'These are forced.' As meticulously staged as a movie production, with numerous characters carefully dressed in costumes, hair and make-up, some of Prager's images took over a year to put together. The polished end result is seductive and destabilising, in part because it isn't absolutely clear *when* we are. Prager's colour palette is classic, her vision impregnated with the memory of Old Hollywood, from Douglas Sirk to Alfred Hitchcock, as well as classical mythology and Dutch Renaissance painting. Her work gives, as Emily Witt writes, 'a feeling of the past without the limitations of historical accuracy'. The image here is further derealised by Prager's post-production editing: she has adjusted it so that all the people in the crowd are staring, but without making eye contact with anyone. Describing her work for the Berlin Biennale in 2022, art historian William J. Simmons calls her crowds 'egalitarian'; each individual contains a story and becomes an archetype. 'They evince that one's fear of being lost – merely one life in a sea of lives – is tragic, beautiful, arduous, a source of unity, and like the photograph itself, replicable.'

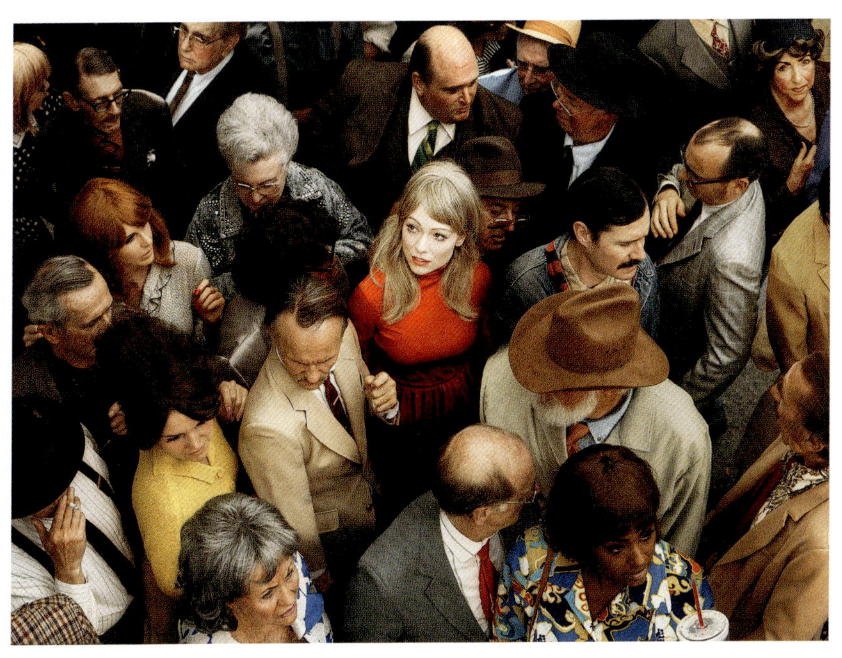

Alex Prager, *Crowd #2 (Emma)*, 2012, 150×205 cm

LORENZO VITTURI

Hairy Orange, Yellow Balloons and Rotten Camote #2, 2014

Multi-ethnic neighbourhood as a modern vanitas

Lorenzo Vitturi's London studio is in Dalston – just up the road from the home of Hoxton Mini Press! In 2014, inspired by the gentrification transforming his neighbourhood, Vitturi decided to document and celebrate the extraordinary diversity of his local market on Ridley Road in the photobook *Dalston Anatomy*, accompanied by a month-long series of performances and installations. The vibrantly colourful sculpture composed in this shot is made from discarded food and other litter he collected from the market. It includes a lemon, pieces of squash and sweet potato (or camote) from South America; a yellow balloon from a Chinese shop (whose shape echoes the lemon's); and an orange wig from one of the biggest afro hair shops in London. Vitturi started out as a film set designer, and his sculptures are carefully built and angled for the camera to capture. Made of perishable organic materials, the structure is ephemeral. Teetering on top of each other like a troupe of acrobats, the objects form an unstable arrangement. For Vitturi, this mirrors the impermanent nature of a rapidly changing neighbourhood, the precariousness of Dalston's mix of cultures threatened by gentrification.

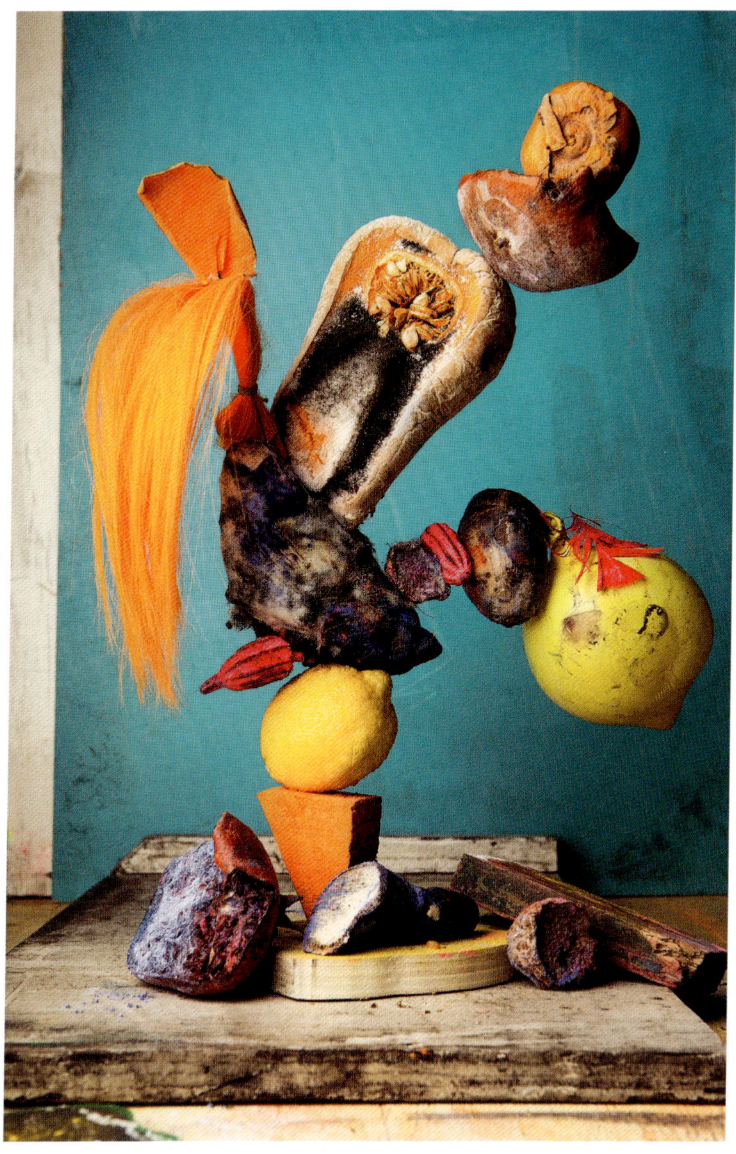

Lorenzo Vitturi, *Hairy Orange, Yellow Balloons and Rotten Camote #2*, 2014

THOMAS SAUVIN

From the series Until Death Do Us Part, 2015

Salvaged picture opens window into life in China

Works by some of the photographers featured in this book have fetched millions of dollars at auction. By contrast, Thomas Sauvin, a French photography collector and editor living in Beijing, purchased images in his *Beijing Silvermine* project at a bulk rate of about $10 per kilo, not from Christie's or Sotheby's but from a recycling plant on the outskirts of the Chinese capital that was using discarded photographic negatives as a source of silver salt. The half-million or so salvaged pictures are in the great tradition of anonymous vernacular photography, documenting the day-to-day lives of ordinary Chinese citizens from the mid-1980s to the rise of digital photography in the new millennium. You might at first mistake this image for a Surrealist set-up, but it captures an authentic wedding custom (albeit one that is now in retreat): the bride is expected to light a cigarette for all the male guests, following which bride and groom indulge in some eye-catching cigarette-based play. Sauvin assembled photographs portraying this tradition into a series smartly entitled *Until Death Do Us Part*, which were then published together in a book designed to resemble a packet of Shuangxi cigarettes – an iconic Chinese cigarette brand.

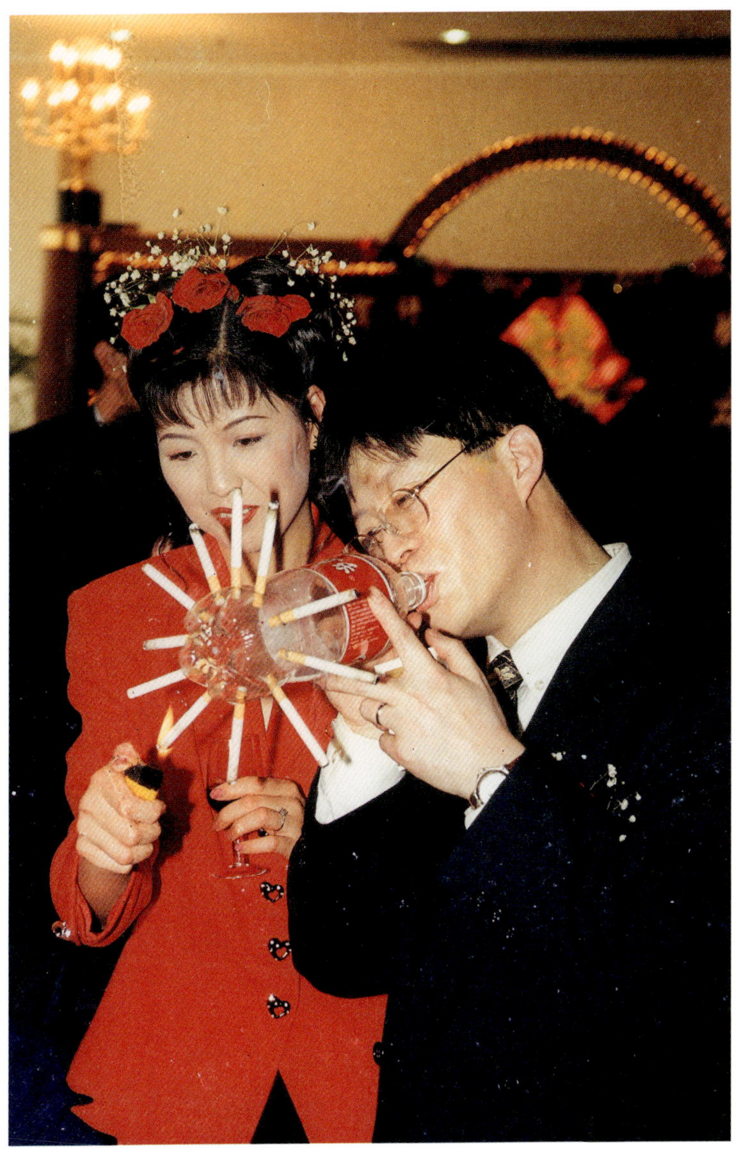

Thomas Sauvin, *Beijing Silvermine, Until Death Do Us Part*, Neg #A-6034-14, 2015

GREGORY HALPERN

Untitled, *from* ZZYZX, 2016

Outsider recasts California as post-apocalyptic dreamworld

Halpern is not a Californian and he brings to the 'Golden State' an outsider's questioning outlook, seeking out elements of strangeness and bleakness under its harsh sun. Taken in the Los Angeles area, from desert to Pacific Ocean, the *ZZYZX* series got its dystopian title from a place on the edge of the Mojave Desert, named by a 'miracle healer' who claimed to have composed the last possible word in the English language. Here, Halpern eschews traditional landscape photography, finding instead a whole psychedelic landscape in the inscrutable back of a man's head. The image plays with stereotypes associated with the American male: the surfer-style glamour of wavy hair delicately bleached blond and pink, trailing frothy hair product, contrasts with the sense of power we receive from the sitter's broad neck and his Mad Max-style leather biker's jacket. In the book, this image is immediately followed by one of the same man's face, looking fiercely intimidating. Whether we see one or both images, Halpern's vision remains open-ended, to be interpreted or simply dreamed about by us.

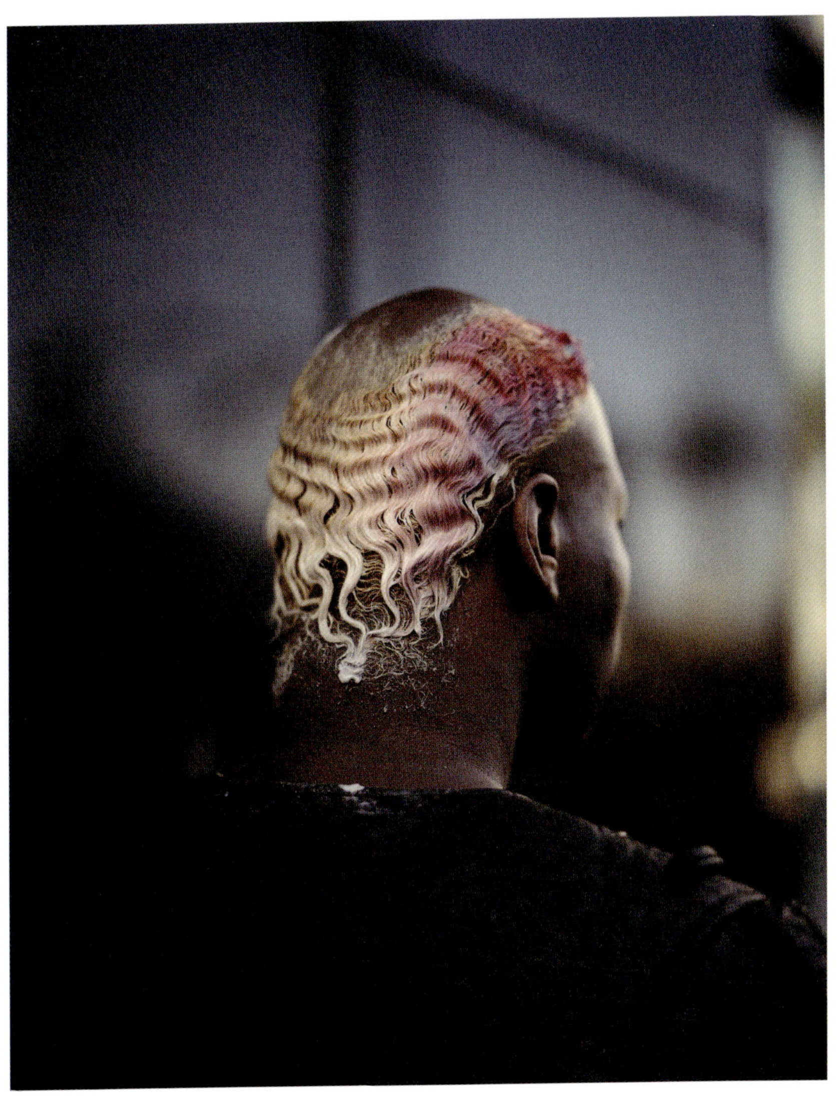

Gregory Halpern, *Untitled*, from the series *ZZYZX*, 2016

JULIE COCKBURN

The Conundrum, 2016

Enigmatic anon picks up the thread

'People often say my work is aggressive, but I think it is the opposite,' British artist Julie Cockburn has said. 'I think it is a loving practice.' She buys discarded vintage photographs of 'almost archetypal ordinariness' from car boot sales and the internet and then, following her instinct to add what seems to her to be missing, completes the images with collage or embroidery in multi-coloured silk threads. At play here is something comparable in spirit to *kintsugi*, the Japanese method of repairing cracked pottery with visible gold. Cockburn's loving defacement of the photograph is carefully prepared: the image is first scanned to allow templates to be made on the computer, an essential step since the image is fragile and will need to be pricked with extreme precision prior to being embroidered. The woman's face has become considerably overlaid with a pattern of silk dots, leaving only one eye free to stare out at us, either pleadingly or indeed watching in safety from behind her new protective screen: therein, perhaps, lies the conundrum.

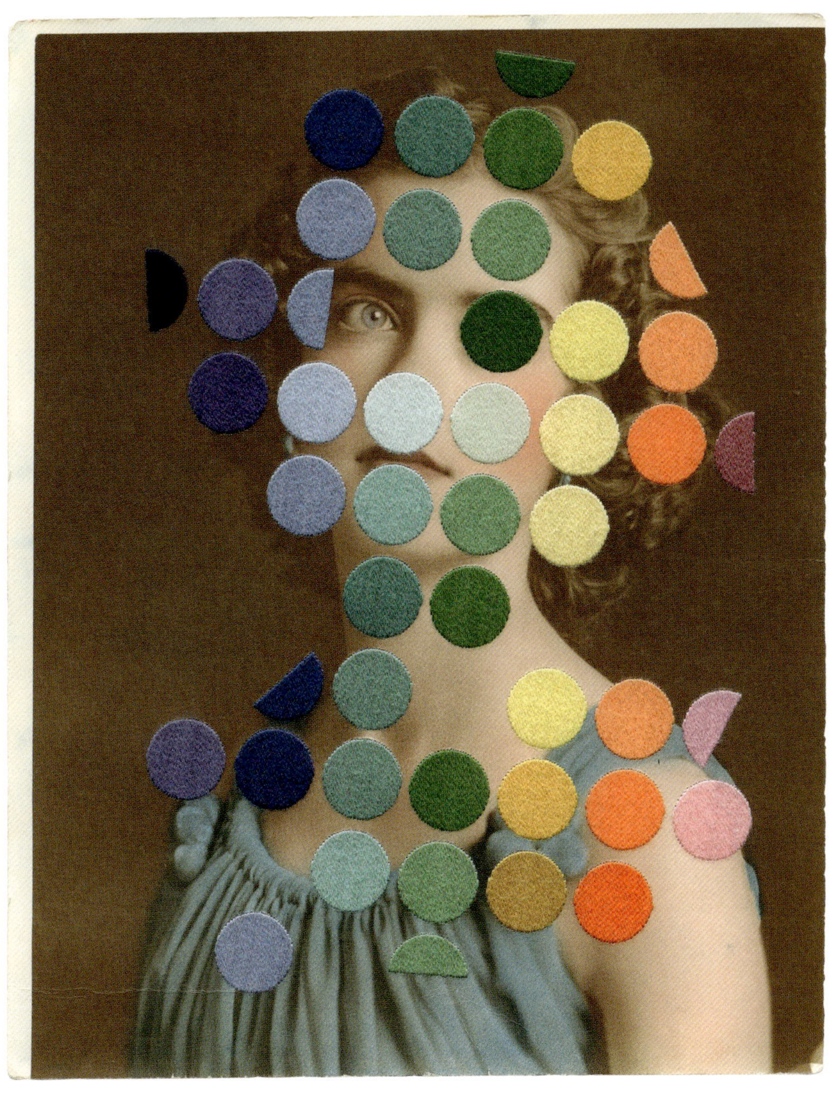

Julie Cockburn, *The Conundrum*, 2016, hand embroidery on found photograph

ZANELE MUHOLI

Ntozakhe II (Parktown), 2016

Black portraiture queered and queried

This is a black-and-white image about colour. South African Zanele Muholi, who identifies as a 'visual activist' rather than an artist, grew up under apartheid. This picture is part of the series *Somnyama Ngonyama* (Zulu for 'Hail the dark lioness'), shot as they travelled around the world and took self-portraits in a variety of theatrical personas, using locally sourced materials – from scouring pads to rubber tyres – as props. The series is a reflection on colonialism, apartheid and stories of racial oppression. It addresses trauma by subverting stereotypes associated with the photographing of Black bodies, offering both a challenging and instructive experience and the possibility of healing. Muholi appears with a crown made of hair doughnuts and a dress reminiscent of Grecian drapery. The references to the Statue of Liberty are deliberate; Muholi asks, 'What is the colour of the Statue of Liberty?' Here the image of the Statue is reclaimed as a triumphantly Black and queer body. In post-production, the artist digitally darkened their skin and whitened their eyes, celebrating Blackness. Muholi resists the assignation of a conventional meaning to a Black body, anthropological or otherwise: the element of masquerade in the image, and throughout the whole series, ensures the preservation of freedom through many assumed personas.

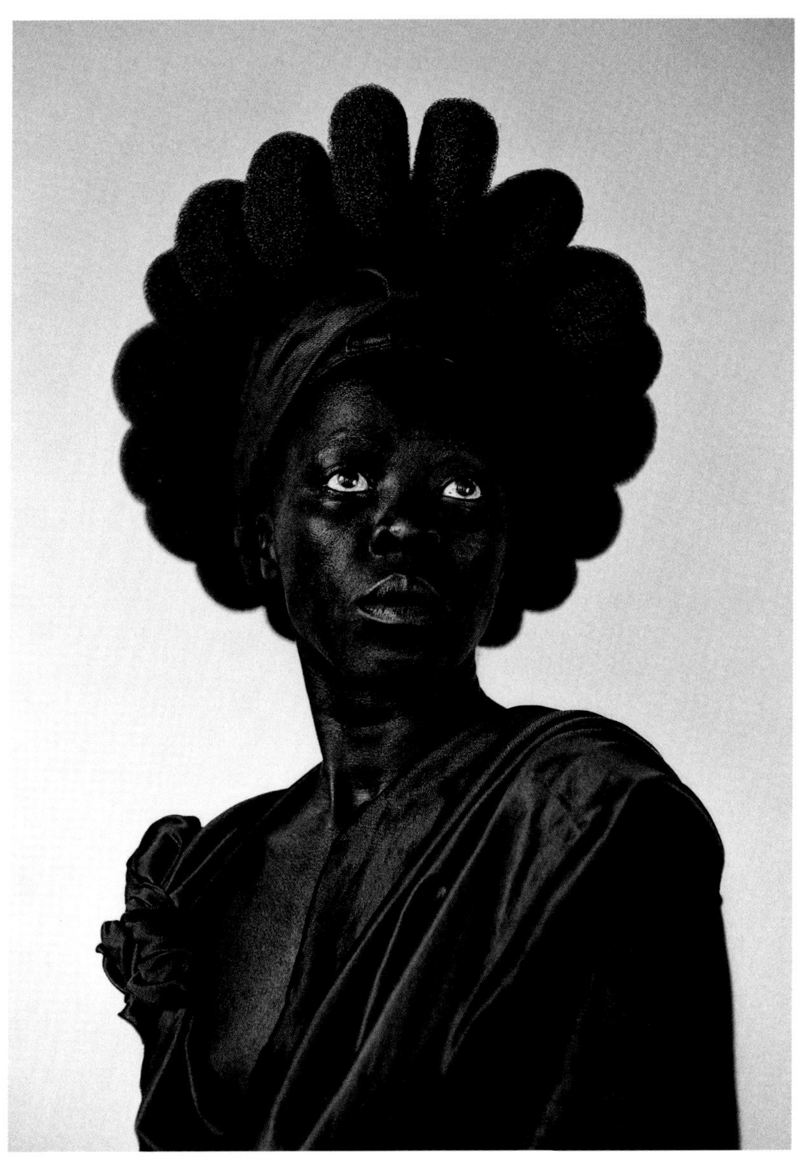

Zanele Muholi, *Ntozakhe II (Parktown)*, 2016

TRENT PARKE

Untitled #7, *from* The Crimson Line, 2019

Industrial reality mutates into ambiguous science fiction

Does this unsettling, majestic image show a prelude to an ecological apocalypse – or is it a magical moment of creation? Reflecting on the colour crimson in his 2019 photobook *The Crimson Line*, Australian photographer Trent Parke points out that it is a colour we can discern through our telescopes at the birth of a star, and one that he also associates with human birth. Meanwhile, he draws a line from the production of crimson dye (made from the crushed bodies of the South American cochineal parasite), mainly used in the food and cosmetics industry, to the sustained industrialisation and pollution of our landscapes, whose effects he records in his photographs of steelworks and chimney fumes. For six months, Parke got up before dawn and shot the first few minutes of sunrise, capturing vivid shades of scarlet, magenta, orange and crimson filtered through the industrial atmosphere in the coastal suburb of Adelaide where he lives. The results are quasi-hallucinatory. Parke's meditative approach is highly cinematic: he is a fan of dystopian science fiction and likes to work to a soundtrack – in this case, the film music of German composer Hans Zimmer, which combines the orchestral with the electronic.

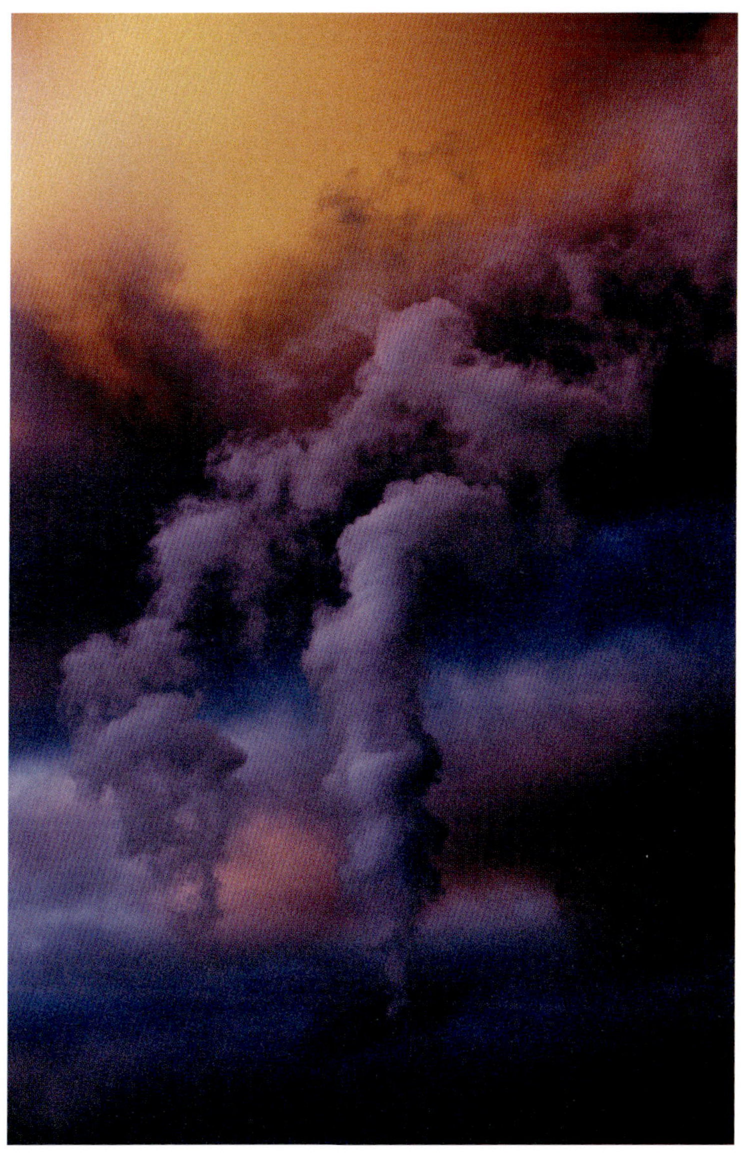

Trent Parke, *Untitled #7*, from *The Crimson Line*, 2019

CHRIS FACEY

From Black Stories, 2020

Every activist is a photojournalist

'When I have my camera on me, I don't forget that I am a Black human being. I remember why I'm at these protests,' said African American photographer Chris Facey, who documented the first Black Lives Matter protests in New York City during the summer of 2020. Facey was determined to tell the story of the protests from the frontline as they unfolded, in order to pre-empt the growth of racist false narratives. But Facey isn't the only one documenting the scene. While the placard pasted with the front page of the *Daily News* functions as an in-built caption for his picture, it does also, as an old symbol of legacy media, recede amid a sea of smartphones. The arms raised in defiance also hold devices recording and instantly disseminating images and sounds from the crowd onto social media. All the subjects in the photographer's picture are photographers, documenting their own experience. Also striking is the presence of masks; Facey's photo was taken at the height of the Covid pandemic. But in the era of CCTV cameras and facial recognition software, what Facey also captures in the protesters' faces is a tension between wanting to bear witness and wishing to remain anonymous.

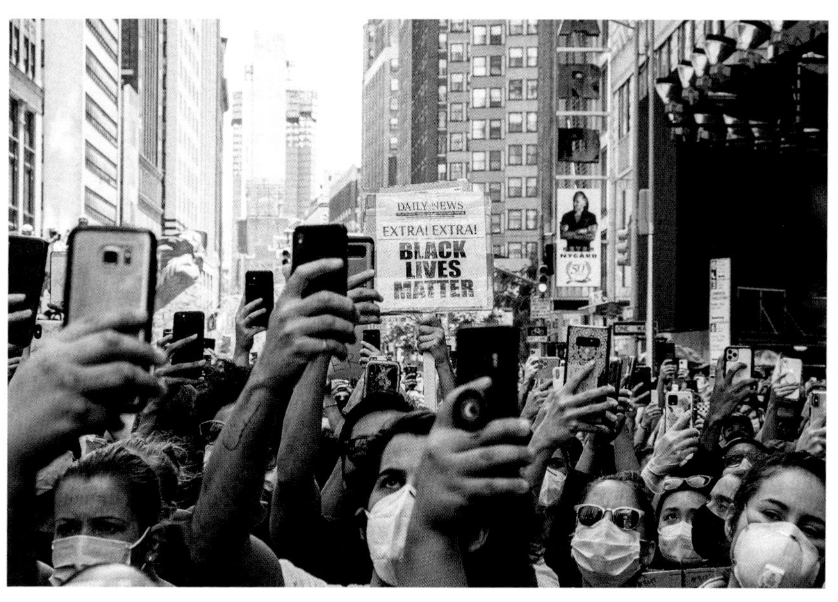

Chris Facey, from *Black Stories*, 2020

BORIS ELDAGSEN

The Electrician, 2022

The woman who wasn't there

This arresting image was entered by its maker – self-styled 'promptographer' Boris Eldagsen – into the prestigious Sony World Photography Awards; it won the top prize in the creative category. Eldagsen turned down the award, revealing that the image had been created with AI and arguing that AI imaging and photography are too different from each other to be considered in the same competition. The rules of the awards did not exclude AI images, perhaps because these had not been thought of as possible entries, but Eldagsen's successful deception of the judges illustrated that a critical turning point had been reached after the 'big bang' of AI image-making software. *The Electrician* is part of Eldagsen's series *Pseudomnesia* ('Fake Memory'), imagined scenes prompted using the visual language of the 1940s. It features flaws of early AI imagery: some fingernails are missing; the pupils of one woman are facing in different directions. Now, such wrinkles can be ironed out. 'The real challenge presented by AI is not that it might rock our attachment to human creativity as somehow unique and unfathomable,' says Eldagsen, who embraces AI image-making as an artist, rather 'the threat is to democracy and photojournalism.' The specificity of what makes an image a photograph needs careful monitoring.

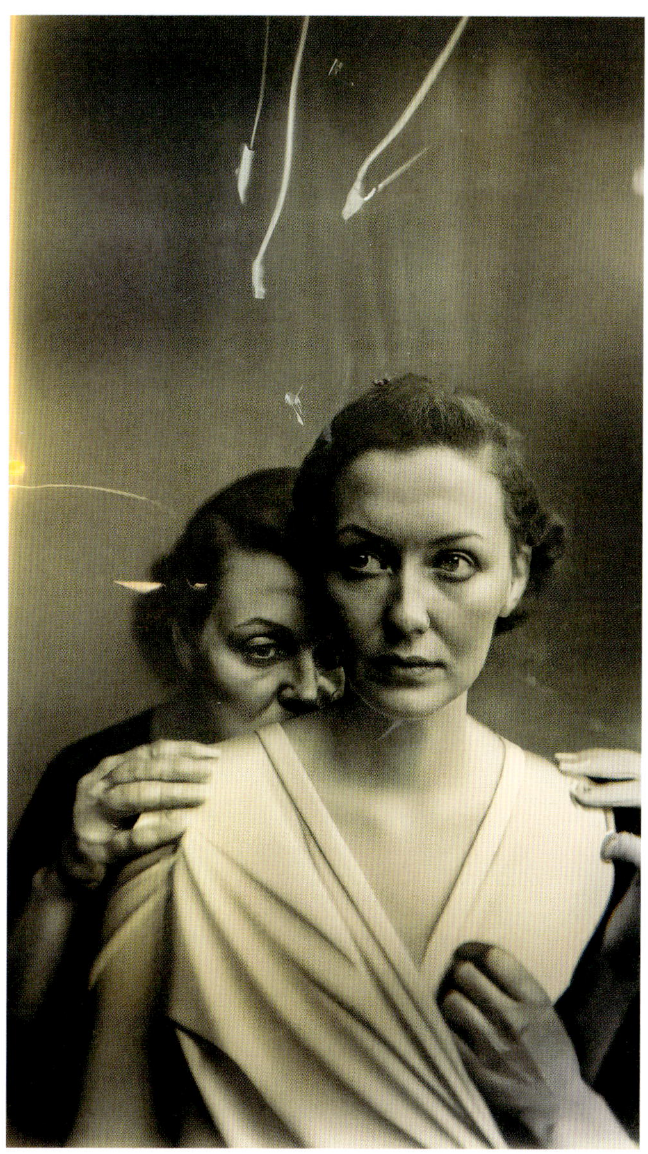

Boris Eldagsen, *The Electrician*, 2022

Artist Directory

Eve Arnold

b.1912, Philadelphia, USA
d.2012, London, UK
Arnold joined Magnum in 1951, after minimal training. In the ensuing 20 years she produced reportage work for magazines, Hollywood portraiture and documentary records of the ex-Soviet Union, Mongolia, China and the Middle East.

Roger Ballen

b.1950, New York, USA
Ballen developed a style of photography through the 1990s which he called documentary fiction, creating powerful psychodramas by photographing marginalised people. He is based in Johannesburg, South Africa.

Guy Bourdin

b.1928, Paris, France
d.1991, Paris, France
Bourdin learned photography during his military service in the air force in Dakar, Senegal. He befriended the Surrealist Man Ray and began to shoot fashion stories for *Vogue* in 1955, coming to prominence at the same time as fellow innovator Helmut Newton. His work is characterised by saturated colour, the suggestion of mysterious, unexplained narratives, and a knowingly perverse mix of glamour and violence.

Bill Brandt

b.1904, Hamburg, Germany
d.1983, London, UK
Brandt is a German-British photographer and photojournalist. After a stint with Man Ray in Paris, he moved to England and documented different aspects of British society for illustrated magazines, as well as the London Blitz for the Home Office. He also explored landscape and nude photography using expressive distortion.

Edward Burtynsky

b.1955, Ontario, Canada
Burtynsky is an advocate for environmental conservation with a distinctive style of large-scale photographs of industrial landscapes illustrating the impact of humanity on nature, simultaneously suggestive of both dread and the sublime.

Claude Cahun

b.1894, Nantes, France
d.1964, St Helier, Jersey
Born Lucy Renée Mathilde Schwob, a French Surrealist photographer and writer who adopted a series of performative and androgynous personae in her self-portraits.

Henri Cartier-Bresson

b.1908, Seine-et-Marne, France
d.2004, Céreste, France
Cartier-Bresson studied painting under Cubist artist André Lhote then pioneered street photography and the idea of capturing a 'decisive moment'. He was a founding member of the Magnum Photos agency in 1947.

Julie Cockburn

b.1966, London, UK
Cockburn trained as a sculptor at Central St Martins in London. Her practice consists of embellishment of found photos with embroidery, painting, cutting and reassembly.

Philip-Lorca diCorcia

b.1951, Connecticut, USA
diCorcia produces meticulously staged photographs of friends and relatives as well as strangers, exploring the tension between artifice and authenticity. He is best known for the series *Hustlers*, in which, against the backdrop of the moral panic that accompanied the AIDS crisis, he photographed male prostitutes in Los Angeles using a government arts grant to pay his subjects.

William Eggleston

b.1939, Memphis, USA
Eggleston is a particularly influential photographer working in colour. He showed an early interest in cameras and then, as a student, came across a copy of Cartier-Bresson's book *The Decisive Moment*. By the end of the 1960s, he photographed predominantly in colour and in 1972 discovered the dye transfer printing technique, which allowed him to produce images of superior colour impact. He documented the transformations of the postwar American South from a predominantly rural to a more suburban society.

Boris Eldagsen
b.1970, Pirmasens, West Germany
Eldagsen studied photography, conceptual art and philosophy and has developed a particular interest in AI-assisted image-making. He has been a member of the Deutsche Fotografische Akademie since 2014 and is based in Berlin.

Chris Facey
b.1990, New York, USA
Inspired by Don Hogan Charles, William Eugene Smith and Roy DeCarava, Facey got into photography in the last years of his service in the US Army. He dedicates himself to documenting Black communities sensitively, rolling back racist stereotypes. He is now based in Raleigh, North Carolina, USA.

Andreas Feininger
b.1906, Paris, France
d.1999, New York, USA
An American photographer and writer on photographic technique, Feininger developed an interest in photography while studying architecture at the Weimar Bauhaus. He moved back to Paris to flee Nazism and worked with Le Corbusier, then to Stockholm and in 1939 to New York. He joined the staff of *Life* magazine in 1943, his subject matter including sculptures, machines and the city. He designed customised telephoto lenses that allowed him to shoot landscapes and city streets in monumental perspective.

Robert Frank
b.1924, Zurich, Switzerland
d.2019, Nova Scotia, Canada
Frank emigrated to America as a young man. His book *The Americans* was the result of extensive travel around the country, and a groundbreaking and profoundly influential photographic account of a socially riven America at the height of the Cold War.

Matt Goins
Goins is a specialist in equine photography, and twice-winner of the Eclipse Prize. He lives and works in Kentucky, USA.

Harry Gruyaert
b.1941, Antwerp, Belgium
Gruyaert made his name on assignment in the 1970s in Morocco and India. He helped to establish colour photography as a respectable visual language and joined Magnum in 1981, the first non-photojournalist to do so.

Andreas Gursky
b.1955, Leipzig, East Germany
Gursky grew up in Düsseldorf, West Germany, where he studied under Bernd and Hilla Becher at the Staatliche Kunstsakademie, learning a detached, documentary style of photography. His subject matter ranges from landscapes to office blocks, and he is known for producing exceptionally large prints, which, sometimes involving digital manipulation.

Gregory Halpern
b.1977, Buffalo, USA
Halpern studied at Harvard and the California College of the Arts. He produced *Harvard Works Because We Do* (2003), a book of photos of the university seen through the eyes of its maintenance employees, and *ZZYZX* (2016), a poetic and dystopian portrait of the Los Angeles area.

Todd Hido
b.1968, Ohio, USA
Hido has an interest in suburban architecture, also portraits, interiors, with home, family and memory as major themes. He lives and works in San Francisco Bay, California, USA.

Nadav Kander
b.1961, Tel Aviv, Israel
A British-Israeli photographer known for his celebrity portrait and landscape photography, particularly his *Yangtze – The Long River* series. Kander is based in London.

Rinko Kawauchi
b.1972, Shiga, Japan
In 2001, Kawauchi simultaneously released a series of three photographic books, *Utatane*, *Hanabi* and *Hanako*, which created an overnight sensation in Japan's photography world. Her work explores the wonder of small things. She lives in Tokyo.

André Kertész
b.1894, Budapest, Hungary
d.1978, New York, USA

Born Andor Kohn. After a 'purist' art photography phase in 1920s Paris, Kertész emigrated to New York in 1936 and freelanced for fashion magazines including *Vogue* and *Harper's Bazaar*.

William Klein

b.1926, New York, USA
d.2022, Paris, France
A French photographer born in New York who moved to photography after studying painting under Fernand Léger. Klein is known for unconventional extensive use of wide angle and telephoto lenses, natural lighting and motion blur in fashion and street photography.

Dorothea Lange

b.1895, Hoboken, USA
d.1965, San Francisco, USA
An American documentary photographer and photojournalist, famous for the photographs she took on behalf of the Farm Security Administration during the Great Depression.

Jacques-Henri Lartigue

b.1894, Courbevoie, France
d.1986, Nice, France
Lartigue's photography captured the allure and *élan* (energy) of upper-class French life. He had a fascination for sport, automobiles, aeroplanes and the dynamism of the human body.

Saul Leiter

b.1923, Pittsburgh, USA
d.2013, New York, USA
Leiter was a photographer and painter. He moved to New York and pioneered colour photography as a fine art in the 1940s–50s, and later worked as a fashion photographer before his work was rediscovered in the 1990s.

Helen Levitt

b.1913, New York, USA
d.2009, New York, USA
Levitt started out as a commercial photographer but began to think of photography as a fine art after befriending Cartier-Bresson in 1935. She spent decades documenting the theatre of everyday street life in New York. An early pioneer of colour street photography, she was also an avant-garde filmmaker and forerunner of cinéma vérité (observational cinema).

Madame Yevonde

b.1893, London, UK
d.1975, London, UK
Yevonde Philone Middleton, née Cumbers was a British photographer and Suffragette who opened her first studio in 1914 as a route to financial independence. An influential artist and innovator and a successful commercial photographer, she created images for illustrated magazines, fashion and advertising.

Vivien Maier

b.1926, New York, USA
d.2009, Illinois, USA
Maier lived as a nanny and carer in suburban Chicago while producing a vast body of work as an amateur photographer of urban life. Her subjects were often children, the elderly and the poor; she also took self-portraits. Her considerable oeuvre was only discovered after her death.

Steve McCurry

b.1950, Philadelphia, USA
An American photojournalist, McCurry has covered many armed conflicts, including the Gulf war, the Iran-Iraq war and the civil wars in Cambodia and Lebanon. He is a frequent contributor to the *National Geographic*.

Joel Meyerowitz

b.1938, New York, USA
Meyerowitz is an American street, landscape and portrait photographer. He has explored colour photography and large format, and was the only photographer granted unrestricted access to Ground Zero to record the aftermath of the 9/11 terrorist attacks on the World Trade Center.

Lee Miller

b.1907, Poughkeepsie, USA
d.1977, East Sussex, UK
Born Elizabeth Miller, Lee Miller was a photographer and photojournalist who worked as a war correspondent for *Vogue* during World War II. She produced a record of the London Blitz, the Liberation of Paris and the Dachau and Buchenwald concentration camps.

László Moholy-Nagy

b.1985, Bácsborsód, Hungary
d.1946, Chicago, USA
An experimental painter,

photographer, sculptor, and professor at the Bauhaus. Moholy-Nagy moved to London in 1935, then Chicago in 1937, where he taught design and made commercial design work.

Daido Moriyama
b.1938, Osaka, Japan
A Japanese photographer whose creative journey has involved radical reinvention, questioning the nature of photography itself, culminating in the 1972 collection *Farewell to Photography*.

Zanele Muholi
b.1972, Umlazi, South Africa
Muholi's childhood was shaped by apartheid and they lived through its abolition. Their photography and video practice centres on overturning anti-Black racist representations and combatting the injustices still faced in South Africa by LGBTQIA+ people by creating positive visual histories, including self-portraits, for under-represented and misrepresented people.

Eadweard Muybridge
b.1830, Kingston upon Thames, UK
d.1904, Kingston upon Thames, UK
Born Edward James Muggeridge, Muybridge emigrated to the USA as a young man. He started his photographic career as landscape photographer of the Wild West, then pioneered chronophotography of animals in motion.

Helmut Newton
b.1920, Berlin, Germany
d.2004, Los Angeles, USA
Born Helmut Neustädter, Newton began his career in fashion photography in the 1950s, when it was a safe, conventional environment. He revolutionised fashion photography and fashion advertising by producing erotically charged, often menacing and powerful images of women.

Timothy H. O'Sullivan
b.circa 1840
d.1882, New York, USA
Born in Ireland or possibly New York, O'Sullivan made his name with photographs of the American Civil War, and later produced remarkable landscape photography, notably of Nevada and the Southwestern United States.

Trent Parke
b.1971, NSW, Australia
Parke began taking photos aged 12. His work provides a physical and psychological portrait of Australia from the Outback to the coast, imbuing reality with poetry and an air of dystopia. He became a member of the Magnum Photos agency in 2007, the first Australian to do so.

Martin Parr
b.1952, Surrey, UK
Parr has taken a particular interest in rural communities and in the behaviour of British social classes, often with a tinge of satire, using close-ups and saturated colour.

Irving Penn
b.1917, Plainfield, USA
d.2009, New York, USA
After abandoning a career in painting, Penn was hired at *Vogue* in 1943, which sent him around the world on fashion and portrait assignments, though he preferred working in the studio. He made the celebrated *Nudes* series as well as the *Cigarettes* series, uncanny 'portraits' of cigarette ends.

Alex Prager
b.1979, Los Angeles, USA
Prager is an American photographer and filmmaker. Influences for her constructed imagined scenes range from the Old Hollywood movies of Douglas Sirk and Alfred Hitchcock to the works of Cindy Sherman.

Man Ray
b.1890, Philadelphia, USA
d.1976, Paris, France
Born Emmanuel Radnitzky, Man Ray was an American artist and photographer who moved to Paris in 1921. Here he rediscovered the process of photograms (cameraless photographs), which he called rayographs in reference to himself, and, with Lee Miller, reinvented the process of solarisation.

Grace Robertson
b.1930, Manchester, UK
d.2021, East Sussex, UK
Robertson was a pioneering female photographer with an interest in documenting the lives of ordinary women. Her subjects were wide-ranging, from

sheep-shearing in Snowdonia to an outing to Margate by a group of women from Battersea in London. Her work was rediscovered in the 1980s.

Sebastião Salgado
b.1944, Aimorés, Brazil
Salgado beecame a photographer in his twenties, firstly as a news reporter, later as a documentary photographer interested in migrants and workers, and more recently in wildlife and landscape. He is also engaged in restoring part of the Atlantic Forest in Brazil.

Viviane Sassen
b.1972, Amsterdam, Netherlands
Sassen lived in Kenya as a child, where her father worked in a polio clinic, and would often play with the young patients. Her work centres almost entirely on Africa, and encompasses high fashion campaigns and fine art photography.

Thomas Sauvin
b.1983, Paris, France
Sauvin is a French photography collector and curator. He started buying negatives in bulk from a recycling plant on the edge of Beijing in 2009, amassing half a million images documenting everyday life in China in his *Beijing Silvermine* project.

Cindy Sherman
b.1954, New Jersey, USA
An American photographer born Cynthia Morris Sherman whose work consists of staged photographs in which she assumes different fictitious identities, evoking female tropes from cinema and beyond.

Malick Sidibé
b.1935, Soloba, Mali
d.2016, Bamako, Mali
Sidibé first trained as a jeweller, then apprenticed as a photographer with Frenchman Gérard Guillat before starting his own career, taking pictures of the youthful Bamako nightlife and later opening his own studio and exploring portrait photography. He was awarded the Golden Lion Award in 2007 for Lifetime Achievement at the Venice Biennale, the first African recipient.

Alec Soth
b.1969, Minneapolis, USA
Soth studied at Sarah Lawrence College in Bronxville, where he was inspired by the work of Diane Arbus. His 2004 book of poetic portraits and landscape photography *Sleeping by the Mississippi* defined his area of interest: Soth is an itinerant photographer, drawn to loners, vagrants and hermits in forgotten parts of America.

Andreas Sterzing
b.1956, Germany
Based in New York for 20 years, Sterzing has documented the East Village and Pier 34 art communities. His work has appeared in publications including *Der Spiegel*, *Marie Claire* and *the New York Times Magazine*. He now lives and works in London and Cornwall.

Hiroshi Sugimoto
b.1948, Tokyo, Japan
A Japanese photographer and architect, Sugimoto studied politics and philosophy in Tokyo and then trained as an artist at the Art Center College of Design in Pasadena, USA. His work examines the way photography tricks the eye through pictures of animal dioramas, historical wax figures and movie theatres.

Larry Sultan
b.1946, New York, USA
d.2009, Greenbrae, California
Sultan grew up in California. As an art student in the 70s, he made conceptual billboards with fellow photographer Mike Mandel. He later documented his parents' retirement in staged photographs published alongside stills from childhood home movies in *Pictures from Home* and the lives of immigrant day labourers in the collection *Homeland*.

Wolfgang Tillmans
b.1968, Remscheid, West Germany
The first photographer to be awarded the Turner Prize in 2000, Tillmans was a chronicler of the London gay and club scenes in the 1990s, then developed interest in experimentation with abstractions, photocopies and 'table works' (collages arranged under glass). He lives in Berlin and London.

Lorenzo Vitturi
b.1980, Venice, Italy
Vitturi is a photographer and sculptor who started out as a film set painter, bringing an element of playful performance and staging to his photographic practice. His project Dalston Anatomy is a series of still lifes and portraits inspired by his local multicultural market in east London. He lives and works between London and Italy.

Ellen von Unwerth
b.1954, Frankfurt, West Germany
Orphaned at an early age, von Unwerth joined a circus in her teens before becoming a model. She took up fashion photography, producing empowering erotic and feminist images within a male-dominated industry. She is based in Paris.

Tim Walker
b.1970, Surrey, UK
Walker is a British fashion photographer. After a brief stint as fourth assistant to Richard Avedon in New York, he began to shoot high-concept stories for *Vogue*, *W*, *i-D* and *Vanity Fair* among others. He has collaborated with musical artists like Björk and Harry Styles. In 2019–20, he staged *Wonderful Things* at the V&A in London, a series of ten installations inspired by artefacts from the museum. He is based in London.

Jeff Wall
b.1946, Vancouver, Canada
Wall is a photographic artist famous for his large-scale backlit photo-transparencies, often staged, and whose compositions often allude to Old Master paintings.

Gillian Wearing
b.1963, Birmingham, UK
Wearing moved to London in 1983, studying at the Chelsea School of Arts and Goldsmiths College, where she became a part of the Young British Artist generation. She uses photography to engage with the lives of others and her own family history. She is based in London.

Alex Webb
b.1952, San Francisco, USA
Webb grew up in New England and studied history and literature at Harvard and photography at the Carpenter Center for the Visual Arts. He became a photojournalist in 1974 and a member of Magnum Photos in 1979. Travelling in Mexico and the Caribbean in the 1970s converted him to the use of vibrant colour. He is based in New York.

Weegee
b.1899, Lemberg, Austria (today Zolochiv, Ukraine)
d.1968, New York, USA
Born Usher Fellig, Weegee emigrated with his family to New York. Started out as a pony ride photographer, then worked in the dark room at photographic agency ACME Newspictures before going freelance in the mid-1930s. He was a pioneer of street crime photography who focused on the dark underbelly of New York.

Edward Weston
b.1886, Illinois, USA
d.1958, Carmel, California
Weston was an American photographer who, after visiting a steel plant in 1922, turned from soft-focus Pictorialism to a greater emphasis on abstract form, pursuing true images of nudes and other natural forms such as dunes and seashells in close-up.

Michael Wolf
b.1954, Munich, West Germany
d.2019, Cheung Chau, Hong Kong
Wolf started work as a photojournalist in 1994, and was based in Hong Kong for eight years, then moved on to fine art photography. He explored subjects such as the Shenzen 'copy artists' who reproduce famous artworks and Tokyo commuters packed in suburban trains.

Glossary

Albumen silver print
Photographic process that played a key role in the development of photography. Paper is coated with egg white (albumen) and sensitised with silver salts to create detailed black-and-white images.

Aperture
Adjustable opening in a lens that controls the amount of light entering the camera, affecting depth of field and determining the sharpness of foreground and background elements.

Art photography
Photographs as a form of visual art, allowing photographers to communicate their unique perspectives and creative vision – unlike commercial or documentary photography, where the main aim is to record or convey information.

Camera obscura
An ancient optical device that projects an external scene onto a surface inside a dark box. Possibly dating as far back as 500BCE, it laid the foundation for the development of modern cameras.

Collage
The combination of multiple images to form an evocative composition. Artists and photographers layer diverse materials such as photographs and magazine cut-outs, sometimes applying other techniques such as embroidery.

Collotype
Photographic printing process that originated in the 19th century, involving coating a plate with a light-sensitive gelatin layer and exposing it to light. The plate is then inked and pressed onto paper, producing high-quality prints.

Composition
Careful arrangement of visual elements to create a balanced, aesthetically pleasing image. Thoughtful composition directs focus and gives impact to photographs.

Dada
Artistic and cultural movement formed during World War I which rejected social and aesthetic convention in favour of satirical and absurd artworks. Dadaist photographers like Man Ray embraced experimental techniques, photomontage and bizarre compositions.

Daguerreotype
Invented by Louis Daguerre in 1839, this was the first commercially successful photographic process, using silver-coated copper plates exposed to light to produce detailed images.

Decisive moment
Coined by Henri Cartier-Bresson, this refers to capturing an instant that reveals the essence of a scene. It emphasises spontaneity and timing, and has profoundly influenced street photography.

Diorama
Intricate miniature scenes that are photographed to appear larger than life. Photographers carefully construct these, playing with lighting and perspective to create fantastical or lifelike settings.

Distortion
Alteration of the natural proportions or shapes of subjects. Distortion can occur accidentally due to lens characteristics or perspective, or it might be deliberately encouraged for visual impact.

Documentary photography
Capturing real-life events, people and environments to create authentic, often powerful, visual narratives. Practitioners include Dorothea Lange and Sebastião Salgado, who use images to bring awareness to global issues.

Dye transfer printing
Colour printing process developed in the early 20th century which transfers separate cyan, magenta and yellow dye layers onto a print, offering great accuracy and richness of colour, especially in fine art photography.

Exposure
This refers to the amount of light reaching a camera's sensor (in digital cameras)

or film. It is manipulated by the use of aperture, shutter speed and ISO settings, and is essential for conveying the intended mood or atmosphere.

Film
Light-sensitive material (usually emulsion-coated celluloid) used to capture and record images. The film reacts to light exposure, producing latent images that can be developed and transformed into photographs through chemical processing.

Film noir
Cinematic genre of the 1940s and 1950s characterised by its dark, shadowy aesthetics. Its moody atmospheres and dramatic compositions transcend cinema and resonate in still images, particularly influencing narrative and street photography.

Kodachrome
Introduced by Kodak in 1935, a colour film renowned for its vivid hues. Discontinued in 2009, it is remembered for its role in capturing iconic moments from the 20th century and was pivotal in shaping the colour photography of William Eggleston, elevating ordinary scenes into vibrant art.

Mise-en-scène
Deliberate arrangement of visual elements within the frame, like theatrical staging, with carefully composed scenes, considered lighting and positioning of subjects to convey narrative, mood and atmosphere.

Modernism
Broad artistic movement that began in the late 19th century and reached its pinnacle in the mid-20th century. Modernist photographers sought to capture the essence of their subjects in new ways, with pioneers like Edward Weston and Man Ray challenging conventions with avant-garde techniques and abstract compositions.

Negative
An inverse image recorded on photosensitive material, usually film or glass, with dark areas appearing light and vice versa. They are used to create 'positive' photographic prints when processed in a darkroom.

Perspective
Capturing a scene from a unique vantage point and influencing how viewers perceive the subject by playing with angles, depth of field and composition in order to tell a story or convey emotion.

Photojournalism
A form of visual storytelling that uses images to record and report current events, usually commissioned by a news outlet. It gives viewers a first-hand look at world events and human experiences through often powerful photographs. A renowned practitioner is Steve McCurry.

Photomontage
Creative technique using different photographic elements to create a single, often surreal, cohesive image. László Moholy-Nagy was an early pioneer, and contemporary practitioners include Jeff Wall and Andreas Gursky.

Photograms
Technique pioneered by Man Ray that allows images to be created without a camera by placing objects directly onto photosensitive material, such as light-sensitive paper, and exposing them to light. The objects block the light, resulting in silhouetted forms when developed.

Pictorialism
Early 20th-century photographic movement that sought to elevate photography into fine art. It championed a painterly aesthetic, moving away from sharp focus and embracing softness and texture to emphasise atmosphere and emotion.

Portraiture
Photographic portraiture originated in the early 19th century, especially with the development of daguerreotypes, as an alternative to painted portraits. Using various techniques and lighting, it seeks to reveal the subject's character and foster a connection with the viewer. Diane Arbus and Irving Penn are among its most celebrated practitioners.

Positive

An image that exhibits the natural tones and colours of the subject, as opposed to a negative, which reverses tones. They are prints from film or digital files and are usually the final viewable image.

Post-photography

The evolving modern-day shift beyond traditional photographic practices, where the boundaries between analogue and digital, and between photography and other mediums, are blurred.

Post-production

Editing and enhancing images after they are captured. Traditionally darkroom techniques such as 'burning' and 'dodging' were used to manipulate images for creative effect; it is now more usual to use software like Adobe Lightroom or Photoshop to adjust exposure, colour balance and sharpness.

Solarisation

Technique pioneered by Man Ray that involves briefly exposing a partially developed film or print to light during processing, creating tonal inversions and producing a surreal, halo-like appearance. It had a huge influence on avant-garde photography.

Staged photography

Deliberate arrangement of subjects and elements within a frame, with carefully planned compositions, lighting and props. It allows for creative storytelling and is favoured by artists including Cindy Sherman and Jeff Wall.

Still life

Art tradition dating back to the Dutch Golden Age, where inanimate objects are arranged to create visually compelling images. Still life photography carefully considers composition, lighting and props to evoke mood, and often celebrates the beauty of everyday items.

Street photography

Photographers roam urban environments, seizing upon spontaneous moments that reveal the authenticity of daily life. The father of street photography was Henri Cartier-Bresson, with renowned modern-day practitioners including Gary Winogrand and Joel Meyerowitz.

Surrealism

The creation of dreamlike or fantastical images by manipulating reality, offering viewers a glimpse into the realms of the imagination. Pioneered by artists like Salvador Dalí and Man Ray, surrealistic photography explores the subconscious, often using techniques such as double exposure and photomontage.

Vanitas

Dutch still-life painting tradition that features symbolic elements, such as skulls and dying flowers, to symbolise the transience of life. Photographers adopt these motifs to create compositions that explore themes of mortality and impermanence.

Vernacular

Images that capture everyday life, often produced by amateurs for personal use rather than for artistic or commercial purposes: snapshots, family albums and candid shots offer glimpses into ordinary moments and cultural histories, as seen in the projects of Thomas Sauvin.

Vogue

American fashion and lifestyle magazine launched in 1892 with 28 international editions including in Britain, France and Italy. Purchased by Condé Nast in 1909 and turned into a women's magazine, and has championed cutting-edge fashion photography since then.

Wide-angle

Lens with a shorter focal length, allowing for a broader field of view to capture more of the scene in a single frame, so largely used for landscapes and architecture. Wide-angle perspectives can also give an immersive feel to photos.

Picture credits

All images © The artists

20: Image © Heritage Image Partnership Ltd / Alamy Stock Photo; *22*: © Ministere de la Culture (France), MMP-AAJHL; *24*: © The Metropolitan Museum of Art/Art Resource/ Scala, Florence; *26*: © RMN-Grand Palais /Dist. Photo SCALA, Florence; *30*: © Henri Cartier-Bresson / Magnum Photos; *32*: © Man Ray 2015 Trust / DACS, London 2024; *34*: © National Portrait Gallery, London; *36*: Scala, Florence/Edward Weston © Center for Creative Photography, Arizona Board of Regents; *38*: © Pictorial Press Ltd / Alamy Stock Photo; *40*: © Bill Brandt Archive Ltd.; *42*: © Weegee (Arthur Fellig) / International Centre of Photography / Getty Images; *44*: © Lee Miller Archives, England 2023. All rights reserved. Photo © Roland Penrose, Lee Miller Archives, England 2023. All rights reserved.; *46*: © The Irving Penn Foundation; *48*: © Andreas Feininger / Getty Images; *50*: © Estate of Vivian Maier, Courtesy Maloof Collection and Howard Greenberg Gallery, New York; *52*: © William Klein Estate; *54*: © The June Leaf and Robert Frank Foundation, from The Americans; *56*: © Grace Robertson / TopFoto; *58*: © Saul Leiter Foundation; *60*: © Eve Arnold / Magnum Photos; *62*: © Malick Sidibé, courtesy Galerie MAGIN-A, Paris; *64*: © The Estate of Garry Winogrand, courtesy Frankel Gallery, San Francisco; *66*: © Eggleston Artistic Trust, courtesy, David Zwirner; *68*: © Joel Meyerowitz, courtesy Howard Greenberg Gallery; *70*: © Stephen Shore. Courtesy 303 Gallery, New York and Sprüth Magers; *72*: © The Guy Bourdin Estate 2018, courtesy of Louise Alexander Gallery; *74*: © Helmut Newton, courtesy Helmut Newton Foundation; *76*: © Cindy Sherman, courtesy the artist and Hauser & Wirth; *78*: © Steve McCurry / Magnum Photos; *80*: © Larry Sultan, courtesy Casemore Gallery, San Francisco; Yancey Richardson Gallery, NY; Thomas Zander Gallery, Cologne; Estate of Larry Sultan; *82*: © David Hockney; *84*: © Daido Moriyama Photo Foundation; *86*: © Film Documents LLC, courtesy Zander Galerie, Cologne; *88*: © Andreas Sterzing, courtesy the artist and PPOW Gallery; *90*: © Philip-Lorca diCorcia, courtesy the artist and David Zwirner; *92*: © Gillian Wearing, courtesy Maureen Paley, London, Tanya Bonakdar Gallery, New York and Regen Projects, Los Angeles; *94*: © Hiroshi Sugimoto, courtesy Frankel Gallery, San Francisco; *96*: © Wolfgang Tillmans, courtesy Maureen Paley, London; *98*: © Martin Parr / Magnum Photos; *100*: Edward Burtynsky, courtesy Flowers Gallery London; *102*: © Todd Hido, courtesy La Galeries Les Filles du Calvaire; *104*: © Jeff Wall, courtesy of the artist; *106*: © Roger Ballen, courtesy the artist; *108*: © Andreas Gursky / Courtesy Sprüth Magers Berlin London / DACS 2024; *110*: © Alex Webb / Magnum Photos; *112*: © Alec Soth / Magnum Photos; *114*: © Ellen von Unwerth; *116*: © Sebastiao Salgado / nbpictures; *118*: © Tim Walker Studio; *120*: © Matt Goins; *122*: © Nadav Kander, courtesy of Flowers Gallery and Howard Greenberg Gallery; *124*: © Michael Wolf Estate, courtesy Flowers Gallery; *126*: © Harry Gruyaert / Magnum Photos; *128*: © Viviane Sassen, courtesy Stevenson Gallery Cap Town, South Africa; *130*: © Rinko Kawauchi, courtesy the artist; *132*: © Alex Prager, courtesy Alex Prager Studio and Lehman Maupin, New York, Hong Kong, Seoul and London; *134*: © Lorenzo Vitturi, courtesy Flowers Gallery; *136*: © Beijing Silvermine; *138*: © Gregory Halpern / Magnum Photos; *140*: © Julie Cockburn, courtesy Flowers Gallery; *142*: © Zanele Muholi, courtesy of the artist and Yancey Richardson, New York; *144*: © Trent Parke / Magnum Photos; *146*: © Chris Facey; *148*: © Boris Eldagsen.

The author would like to thank his mentor, Dr M.A.Y. Zagha

An Opinionated Guide to Photography
First edition

Published in 2024 by Hoxton Mini Press, London

Text by Robert Shore
Editing by Octavia Stocker and Florence Ward
Design by Tom Etherington
Additional design and production by Richard Mason
Proofreading by Gaynor Sermon

A CIP catalogue record for this book is available from the British Library.

ISBN: 978-1-914314-62-9

Printed and bound by Finidr, Czechia

Hoxton Mini Press is an environmentally conscious publisher, committed to offsetting our carbon footprint. This book is 100 per cent carbon compensated, with offset purchased from Stand For Trees.

Every time you order from our website, we plant a tree:
www.hoxtonminipress.com

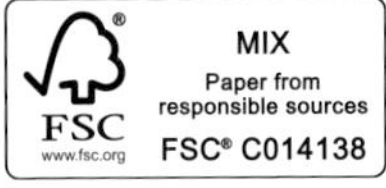